C000096652

First E

Disclaimer and copyright.

Foreword - *Ione Butler, Uplifting Content*

As founder of Uplifting Content, (www.upliftingcontent.com), it has been my mission to uplift people and inspire them to make positive changes in their lives and for others.

90% of news that we see is negative and yet amazing things are happening in the world every day and incredible people doing great things for others and by sharing those stories we are reminded of the good in humanity and the good in ourselves.

"Ask Frankie, The Future You", is unique in several ways - firstly, it has an absolute focus on helping people to be the best that they can be. Quite often people get depressed or down because they are unhappy with certain aspects of their life. Part one contains 5 steps that a person can follow in order to identify what they would like to change, with a plan and structure to follow. It is a fun and exciting way to plan your life.

Secondly, it creates an accountability partner - that partner being the reader, but in the future. It makes the reader accountable to themselves and with downloadable material to help plan and track their progress, it is extremely easy to follow.

The second part of the book gives practical tips and advice on how to deal with challenges, such as stress, anxiety, procrastination and ultimately how to be happier.

There is a recommended daily routine that can assist with all the above. I believe that following the guidance in this book can help to dramatically improve the reader's life which is very much aligned with my work at 'Uplifting Content.' I wish you every success in the journey on which you about to embark.

Kind Regards
Ione Butler.
www.upliftingcontent.com

Foreword – Gareth (Author)

Thanks for making the investment and putting your trust in us. The main goal of Ask-Frankie is to help people achieve the lives that they want. We have worked on this for several years and finally, we are proud to say, it is now complete.

Ultimately, we want to help you to make decisions with consciousness, proactively planning and not just to drift through life reacting to the decisions being made for us. Are you happy with your life currently? Are there any areas that you would improve if you were given the chance? Most importantly, could you have made different decisions over the last 5 years, that would have resulted in you being in a better place now?

Our purpose is twofold. Firstly, it is a good repository for us to collate the information that we have learnt over the years, and secondly, both Steven and I like to help people. We honestly believe that you can change your life in any way that you wish and that it can be quick and simple to achieve. For every decision you make, you need to be conscious every time, not just get tied up in life – but think about each decision because that is what makes the difference.

Most of us live life in a bit of a rat race, getting caught up with everyday life without ever stopping to take stock. The period of lockdown we faced in 2020 and 2021, for me was the first time in my 20-year career where I had longer than 2 weeks away from work at one time, but more importantly, the first time where I was forced to cut myself off from work due to the furlough rules. In the past, even on holiday, I would be constantly checking my emails and replying/working.

That period was a real eye-opener for me. That complete break from the stresses of everyday working life and living in the present moment gave me time to think and to take stock of what is important in life.

Throughout the book we refer to several resources and books that we recommend – these have played a part in building our thoughts and beliefs which have given rise to this book; these can be found in the resources section.

The book comprises 2 parts as explained below. Co-Author Steven says *"We have been back and forth over which part should come first because they are 2 very different formats. Part 1 is a lot more about 'doing' and researching; finding yourself.*

Part 2 is around education and interesting statistics to get you thinking. I would say, that if you raring to go, to change and create that plan now – go straight to Part 1. If however, you are currently a little overwhelmed and in need of some guidance and ways to be happier and more relaxed, then start with Part 2. Either way – just start…..now. Enjoy and good luck"

Part 1
Frankie is, in essence, you….the future you. We describe this concept in more detail and how to use this character as an accountability partner.

We also introduce you to the team of advisors. These are aspects of you, and they can help you to make conscious decisions.

We then look at your previous 5 years, using examples of Frankie, to see the impact of your previous decisions and choices. We have downloadable tools to aid/assess this and I think you will be surprised as to how slight changes can make significant differences in a very short time.

Then we move on to the really fun part – designing the next 5 years, based upon the valuable insights you have discovered, with tangible facts and figures that allow you to quantify how small changes can make such a significant difference.

Lastly, we show you how to regularly monitor and review these goals and aspirations to help you to stay on track.

Do you want the next 5 years to yield the same results as the previous 5? I am guessing not, otherwise, perhaps you would not have invested in this book. Commit to follow the steps here and see the difference this delivers.

Part 2

This part is completely different to part 1 and can help you with key issues that you may be facing such as anxiety, negative thinking, achieving happiness, and focuses on the planning of a daily routine.

We aim to try to convey exactly how we live and how we try to be the best we can be and achieve happiness. The important point throughout is that happiness is not in the destination but in the journey. This has become quite a cliché now, however, if you take note of the message it is an especially important one.

"Happiness is not the destination, but the journey."

If you are about to watch a film and someone tells you the ending, are you still as keen to watch it? No, because the ending is only a part of it – you enjoy the journey, the whole film. Similarly, you would never just watch the ending of a film, for similar reasons – it would not make sense and the journey would be lacking.

For that same reason, would you ever just read the last chapter of a novel?

Downloads.

Throughout the book, there are various resources that we refer to which are free for you. You can download these at the following website:

www.ask-frankie.com

Simply register and you will receive an email with the download link.

How to use the resources

Download these files to a location on your computer and follow the instructions in this book as to what to use and when.

There are 2 copies of each, a PDF for printing if you prefer to use pen and paper, and the source file, allowing you to change and adapt these to your requirements.

We have also put all the templates into a second, diary-style book, details of which can be found on Amazon.

All that remains is for us to wish you the best of luck.

Go on – get going – let us change Frankie together.

Gareth Lewis

Table of Contents

Today marks the beginning of an exciting journey for you – a journey to the best life that you can imagine. Shortly we are going to introduce you to your team - you are going to be working closely with this team for the rest of your wonderful life – but first, we want to just set the scene.

What does a wonderful life look like? We liken it to a cake – you need all the ingredients, in the correct measure, to make it a success. If any one of these ingredients are of the incorrect measure or missing, then this will give you a different outcome to what you want to achieve.

Your life is much like that, you could have all the money in the world, but without your health, what do you have really?

We have aimed to create a concise book, one which can be consumed in one sitting should you wish. So many self-help books exist which never really give specific instructions on exactly how to achieve the dreams that are detailed within the pages. Let us say they 'dangle but don't deliver'.

This book is different – it is a method of managing your mind, with the use of your team, to make conscious decisions in every area of your life. We intend to keep it simple and not bombard you with "big words" to justify the book – less is more.

Who is Frankie?
So, you may be wondering who Frankie is – well, we want to tell you a story to give context to the advice that we are putting forward and as a result, we wanted to base this around a character. To avoid any bias towards gender, we thought it worth giving the character a gender-neutral name, and so 'Frankie' was born.

Frankie is you – only the "Tomorrow You". This is you in 1 second, hour, week, a month from now. We are going to go on a journey with Frankie, discussing where Frankie has been and where Frankie wants to be. Frankie is the real you – not the ego that drives your conscious mind, it is the real you behind that and we are going to discover Frankie together.

When we refer to ego, we are talking about the conscious part of you, that makes decisions purely out of vanity or desire. It is defined as "a person's sense of self-esteem or self-importance" (Oxford Dictionary).

Next, however, we discuss the 5-step plan – that's is right, to achieve anything that you want in life, you need to follow just 5 steps – in the order that they are communicated - that's it, simple eh?

Part 1 – Frankie – Past, Present and Future

The 5 Step Plan

> "Success will never be a big step in the future; success is a small step taken just now"
> Jonatan Martensson

The five steps are amazingly simple for you to follow. We encourage you to read them first in full. Then armed with the knowledge of what you are trying to achieve, read the rest of the book.

We are taking a little bit of a risk by presenting the concept ahead of the context (this is usually done in the reverse) but we thought that you, like us, would want to get this done first. The chapters that follow introduce you to the key concepts that will give meaning to the 5 steps as well as touch on some other key areas where your mind, attitude and drive can help you.

So, the 5-step plan is as follows:

1 – Meet the Team.
>   This is your unique team of advisors who will guide you from this day onwards. You will find out who they are in the next section, but rest assured, you already know them. They attempt to guide you every day, you are just largely oblivious to them or you have not taken the time to listen to the messages that they are trying to give you.

2 – Assess your last 5 years.
>   This will become clearer once you have read the short but very concise story of the real Frankie.

3 – The next 5 years
>   Do not worry, it is not about strict plans and budgeting. In time this will become second nature anyway. This step is all about deciding what you want to achieve in the next 5 years, based upon what you have learnt from step 2.

4 – Write your story.
>   When you commit to paper, you commit. This is a seriously fun part and enables you to dream big for your future.

5 – Assessment
>   Keep track of progress and plan whilst seeing the achievements you have made.

And that is it – the 5-step plan, simple and easy to follow – we have created the free resources that you require, and they are available to download here – just register and receive the download instantly.

http://www.ask-frankie.com/

They are free for you to print and reproduce as much as you like. We have also produced a diary format which is also available from Amazon.

So, without further ado, let us go ahead to Step 1 of the plan and meet your coaches – the team who are going to help and advise you on all areas of your life.

Meet the Team

"Don't wait for something to happen, make it happen"
Colin Schabenbeck

The members of your team are your advisors and confidants. Most importantly they work for you. Their role is to be firm, but fair. They will not always be your friend, but they can be supportive when necessary.

It is your task to construct these team members in your mind, they can be anyone you like, made up, or based upon people that you know and trust. Alternatively, people you don't know but are aware of perhaps.

It is their purpose to be objective and independent. They are not 'yes' people. They will at times remain aloof and at arm's length, devoid of emotion and physical attachment. Create characters and settings for role-play meetings. These need not be real people, just characters to imagine. Importantly, however, they will offer constructive advice and encouragement. So, they will need to remain objective and pragmatic; they are removed from the situation and can therefore apply a clear vision from an independent point of view.

When constructing these people in your mind, you should think of the kind of traits necessary to deliver the support and advice that you seek from each role. Visualise that person, perhaps it is a parent, or a friend, someone from work, perhaps it is even a finance director or banker that you know. Or maybe this person is no longer with us, but someone whose opinion you valued, or someone whose approval you seek. Someone you would like to make proud, perhaps. Or someone that you have made up, carrying traits from multiple people – the choice is yours.

In any case, try to consider the personality traits required of each person and practice this role. This will be instrumental in how well-orchestrated your internal dialogue or role-play sessions will be. Exactly how you construct these people in your mind is not so important nor is how you create the sessions or when or where you do it.

What is important is that you make time for these sessions and make them work for you, perhaps blocking out 1 hour per week in your calendar for "Personal Time". Visualising them is important and the more vivid they are the better. Above all, make it personal to you. No one else needs to know the detail.

Create characters in your sessions based upon real people that you respect, whose opinions you value and whose approval you seek. Consider how they might respond to you and the advice they will give. Be honest. Be constructive. Have fun. But keep it focused.

The chosen Individuals and their character traits will be dependent largely upon your goals. If you are seeking financial orientated objectives, you will have a more analytical focus and methodical view of finances, whereas if seeking weight loss and dietary objectives, you will have a more health-focused agenda.

When seeking to further your education, build your career, or engage in charitable work, you will steer towards legacy aspects. Finally, if you are aiming to overcome addiction or improve decision making, you may explore personal choices and focus primarily on moralistic aspects.

We imagine that overall, you will be seeking some inclusion of several or all of these four main elements just described. There will be some cross-over and instances where your goals are interlinked, and you will seek a balance that fits your goals and suits your personality traits.

Be Creative
Of course, our journey is unique to each of us. We are all seeking different outcomes for ourselves and there is no 'one-size-fits-all'. You may wish to attach your own titles and introduce your own characters, rather than those suggested. That is fine, whatever works best for you. In fact, the more you personalise this and make it your own, the better.

Now, from your downloads complete "The Management Team"

Add an extra dimension to your 'meetings' by adding imagery. It can help if you can visualise their faces. The more creative you can be, the more it can help.

Meeting Location
We encourage you to find your own quiet, happy place, wherever works best for you. Once you have the hang of it, it will become second nature. Some of us may prefer to do this outside, in our garden or in a public park. Again, there are no set rules. Instead, what is important is what works best for you.

At university, I used to travel to the Lake District, to Grasmere, and sit for hours at the boat house on the lake, studying my notes ahead of exams. I found this incredibly conducive to learning. Try to find your special place. I go to this place regularly both physically and in my mind, remembering the sights and the smells. Find your happy place.

This boathouse and other videos can be viewed at either
https://www.facebook.com/thefutureyou1 or
https://bit.ly/3gJhUV6

When considering the setting, again think about what works best for you. If you have an entrepreneurial or business background, you may wish to hold official 'board meetings' with your directors/advisors. You may prefer a different approach, perhaps discussing with your advisors in a therapy session, or you may find solace around a meeting table in a staff room; the choice is very much yours, there are no rules here, just advice.

"What is important is that you have this internal discussion and embrace the process."

Together we are creating your accountability partner – you, just in the future. Consciously making decisions based upon advice from your advisors; really considering your choices.

At first, this process may seem a bit strange, even bizarre, but as with so much in life, we get out what we put in. So, make it personal, embrace it and enjoy it, after all, it is your journey.

Generally, we all have people in our lives who we look up to, turn to for advice, seek praise from, seek approval from, offload to and share experiences with. We do not go through life alone. The process of setting your goals should be no different.

So, let us now introduce the people with whom we will embark on this exciting journey. Let us meet our advisors and confidants.

Finance Coach/Mentor

- Highly measurable. Short and Long-term goals.
- Goal specific.
- Easy to 'SEE' the benefits. Easy to measure success.
- Some willpower, restraint and possibly some action will be required.
- Black and white goals (clear), objective not subjective.
- Not so easy to 'cheat' or fool oneself.
- Still need to be firm.
- The setting of clear miniaturised goals.
- Calculable targets.

The purpose of this person is to be a sounding board as well as a guide – consulting with this person for decisions around spending or saving money. Ideally, if you have someone who you would normally ask on this subject for the larger spend, visualise them and ask them the questions in your mind. What would they say?

This accountability can drastically change spending habits if you are consciously 'checking in' with an advisor ahead of buying anything, large or small; considering the purchase based upon what this person would say, rather than just aimlessly carrying on, can give you a vast amount of power and control.

If you have ever bought something and told someone "but don't tell my Dad, Mum, Sister....." etc – then this person is probably the ideal candidate for this role and consult with them when making this decision albeit imaginary.

Health Coach/Mentor

- A friendly, caring, concerned family doctor.
- Firm taskmaster, (old PE teacher).
- Assertive Sergeant Major type.
- Supportive personal trainer.
- Motivator.
- Keep you focused.
- Does not overlook the detail.
- It will require willpower.
- Goal orientated, but not quite so black and white, a little more subjective than financial goals. Should try to focus on measurable, quantifiable objectives.
- To keep an eye on the prize.
- To focus on the result.
- To visualise the body and health you want.

You would consult with this person on everything health-related. From dietary advice to exercise, from bad habits to mindfulness. This person wants a balanced approach, moderation and exercise is the order of the day. Who this person is will depend on what you want to achieve – it could be a mix of the above attributes but if you want to get up at 6 am every day to go running, you will want more of the Sergeant Major type in this role.

Again, if you can relate this to someone that you know or know of, with the key attributes that you can add to, this is ideal. With all the advisors, your goals need to drive their behaviour and their guidance back to you.

Morality Coach/Mentor

- Perhaps a fairy godmother character, family member or friend.
- The moral compass.
- A practical and sensible friend.
- Imagine running your proposed actions by your family and friends, would you be comfortable doing this?
- Your real conscience.
- Self-critical and self-aware.
- This is perhaps the least measurable element of all the advisors/coaches.
- Requires a greater level of self-control and restraint.

Some additional questions that this coach may raise in your mind or ask you at the point of all decisions:

- Are you betraying anyone?
- How would you feel if you were being asked this by a friend?
- Are you letting yourself or someone else down?
- Could things be done in a different/ better way?
- Requires constant reviewing and setting of goals.
- Maybe an element of soul-searching.
- Imagine yourself in the third person.
- Picture yourself in 5 years: Jail, hospital, morgue.

This is the easiest to explain but the hardest to measure – on the basis that we are all connected and harming someone ultimately means you are harming yourself; you should always aim to do the right thing.

Legacy Coach/Mentor

- This mentor is concerned with how you are perceived.
- It also is about what you want your life to be about.
- What do you want to leave behind for your kids, the human race?
- Is your decision moving you towards or away from this moral standpoint?
- This coach is there to consider whether you are working towards a goal of achieving something long-lasting.
- One task the mentor will ask of you is to write your obituary (a long time in advance – we hope!). More on this later.
- Longer-term goal orientated.

Some questions to consider that this mentor may raise in your mind when making decisions:

- Write down your own commandments.
- Are you being mindful of what you want to leave behind?
- How will you be viewed?
- Think about your social [media] footprint?
- Goals to live towards
- Do not be too hard on yourself – small steps.
- Consider it a journey.

What do you want to achieve in your life and what difference can you make? What are your commandments and your rules to live by? Perhaps write them down.

A quote that I love is by Mahatma Gandhi:

"Be the change that you want to see in the world".

Do not sit and complain about how bad your life is or how bad the world is – go and change it. If you do not at least try, you have no grounds to complain. Be mindful that you will not achieve all the points every time and you may need to keep revisiting these commandments. We should keep reminding ourselves of these until they become embedded in our subconscious and we start to become this better person naturally.

The elements we have described are in many cases inter-linked and we believe that without all of them, you cannot be genuinely happy. Remember life is a journey, not a destination. So, remember to have fun along the way. Do not wait until you get there, as the journey's end will always be extended.

Recognise all the joy and happiness as the events occur and please be aware, these events are not always like the postcards that you may be imagining now. Give yourself praise and enjoy small rewards along the way.
- Be realistic.
- Keep goals achievable.
- Leave room for manoeuvre.

If you believe that the end goal will make you happy, consider this. How many wealthy, fit, healthy, people with flash cars and huge homes have sadly taken their own lives?

How many people at the top of their career have sought consolation in drugs and alcohol? This is often because their happiness is dependent on an end goal which, once achieved, is replaced by another. Think about buying a new car – the anticipation is a wonderful feeling and then receiving delivery or collecting from the garage is also wonderful. Fast forward a month when the first bill payment comes in – are you still quite as happy? Really? Not even 1% less happy?

The answer is probably no, you aren't quite as happy – so the item itself did not bring you happiness but your thoughts around it – it is therefore important to try and achieve that frame of mind every day – and you can with greater control over your mind which this plan can assist you with.

We suggest that you access the resources for free at the website and make them your own. Do what you need to, change, adapt, use, scribble over them – the choice is yours. This is the team that is going to guide you for the rest of your wonderful life.

Remember, happiness needs to be on the journey and not solely in the destination.   Otherwise, when you have reached that destination you will then be looking towards the next one, and then the next one after that until you run out of destinations, and happiness is therefore ultimately impossible.

Do not forget our analogy about a film – you don't watch a film purely for the ending – if you did, you would just watch the ending. You enjoy the whole film (journey) and the end point (your goal) is merely a part of that journey.

"If you change the way you look at things, the things you look at change". *Wayne Dyer*

Writing your obituary

"Always be a first-rate version of yourself, instead of a second-rate version of someone else"
Judy Garland

Do not let life fly past without doing anything meaningful, really think about your message to the world.

Mahatma Gandhi had many wise words and a fantastic outlook on life. One story involved a reporter chasing him through a train station to get an interview. Gandhi boarded the train and as it pulled out, the now desperate reporter shouted:

"Sir, Sir, please, a message for your people!" and Gandhi replied, smiling:

"My life is my message".

Take some time to think about this. Every day you are communicating your message to the world – make it a good one.

At your funeral, when people are reading out words about you, what would you like them to say?

> "Well, they were pretty miserable most of the time, gossiping about all the bad things that they had heard and weren't that much fun to be around. They always wanted what others had and had an unbelievable ability to turn a positive into a negative." Perhaps someone would not say this publicly of course – but would they think it?
>
> OR
>
> "Frankie could not do enough for other people – whenever I needed a shoulder to cry on, laugh, chat through a new idea or anything else, they were always there. They could fall into a hole of mud and find a positive out of it! They had such a positive impact on my life."

Now, these are 2 short examples, but have some fun with this – write down exactly what you want people to think of you, what you achieved and how you made people feel – you then have a blueprint of your life from now until then.

Writing Your Obituary
Write this down in a notebook, a computer or somewhere safe and refer to it regularly. Change it regularly too, your goals and your view of the world will change as time passes, especially if you take notice of the points we raise in the second part of this book. Do this now – before going any further.

Have you done it? Go on, do not go further until you have – it is both difficult but insightful to see how you want to be known or remembered and only then can you assess how closely you are aligned to this.

Well done, that is not always easy to do – but can you see how focusing on the end goal can mean a change in the way you live your life? The above is a blueprint for how you should live your life – you want people to think of you this way, so be that person, every day.

Now you have a better idea as to what you want your message for the world to be, it is time to learn a little more about Frankie. This will give you a good understanding of how you can analyse your decisions over the last few years and identify where changes could have been made.

Frankie's Story

"It is never too late to be what you might have been"
George Eliot

Let us begin by firstly looking at the last 5 years and then forward to the next 5.

The Last 5 Years
So, what has Frankie been up to for the past 5 years? 5 years is an especially important time frame as it will form the basis of the future you for the next 5 years.

Frankie is an adult who, 5 years ago to this very day, embarked on the journey that you are about to undertake. Here is what Frankie had done during the previous 5 years.

Frankie had worked in a job that they did not really like, but it "paid the bills". Frankie had quite an active social life, did little in the way of exercise or self-education and was destined to stay on this track forever. Frankie was averaging just 4000 steps per day and consumed a minimum of 1600 calories per day.

Let us start by looking at what the Coaches/Mentors would say.
- Finance
    - You are being very generous to others which is nice, but perhaps start to think about the future.
    - Spending too much on things you do not need.
    - Saving nothing for a secure future.
- Health
    - You have recently started the Couch to 5K, keep this up.
    - Bad habits are killing you, alcohol for example.
    - You do less exercise than you tell yourself or others.
    - Overall lack of exercise is not good for you.
    - You know which foods are better for you but are eating Junk far too regularly.
- Morality
    - You obey laws and never act immorally which is great.

- o Your life could be viewed as selfish, due to self-indulgence.
- Legacy
  - o Except for potentially completing one of the box sets or computer games, you are going to leave this life without having achieved anything or left any form of legacy.

We can all see that the above lifestyle is not a good one. Satisfaction will not be achieved, and that dead-end job is going to be there forever with no prospects of moving on or starting a business for example.

Frankie decided at that point to change their life, the results were staggering.

Here are some of the changes that Frankie made:
- Reducing unnecessary spending
- Walked an additional 6,000 steps per day.
- Spend 1 hour per night on personal education, online courses or planning the business they had always wanted to start.
- Reduce calories by 100 per day.
- Take responsibility for their current life and write down 3 items per day that they are grateful for.

The Next 5 Years

Frankie stuck to all these changes for the following 5 years – what you may be surprised to hear is that on the health elements alone, Frankie walked an additional 10,950,000 steps over 5 years – 182,500 fewer calories – what does all this equate to?

Did you know:

> "**A** pound of fat equals 3,500 **calories**. Shaving **100 calories** each **day for** 365 days is roughly 36,500 **calories**, equivalent to 10 pounds of pure fat. **You could** double your weight loss to 20 pounds in **a** year by trimming **100 calories** from your diet and burning **100** extra **calories** each **day**" - Onhealth.com

This is equivalent to 50lb per year!

AND

> "Studies show that **running** just **5 to 10 minutes** each **day** at a moderate pace may help reduce your risk of death from heart attacks, strokes, and other common diseases. But the same research also shows that these benefits top off at 4.5 hours a week, meaning there's no need to **run** for hours each **day**"
> **Healthline.com**

As part of the coach/mentor meeting, Frankie wrote down 5 ideas per week of possible business ideas – resulting in one idea being viable, and Frankie sought investment from the bank who matched their investment resulting in Frankie having the capital to start a business which is now making considerable returns for Frankie.

Financially Frankie is way better off, has lost considerable weight and is now at their goal weight, their health is soaring, and they spend their life being grateful for what they have – this "attitude of gratitude" is making Frankie be the person they want to be – people want to be around them as Frankie makes them feel good about themselves.

Every week Frankie reads the obituary they wrote on day one and uses this as a compass to ensure they are progressing and growing every day. Frankie enjoyed the exercise so much that it led to running more regularly and they have recently completed the London marathon – not bad for a self-confessed porker just 5 years ago.

"Little changes over a sustained period bring changes that are sustainable vs a big bang change in lifestyle that soon becomes tiring."

You may be thinking, OK, good for Frankie, but how does this make any difference to my life – come on, stop with the negative attitude - don't you realise **you are** Frankie? Well, maybe not the one in the example, but whatever it is that you want to achieve in life, you can; simply change your outlook, the plan that you are following, and you can make a difference.

Like most people, you may feel you are muddling through life accepting that this is all there is ever going to be – you are making decisions on autopilot without really thinking about your actions. We are going to change this together and create an individual blueprint for your life that, when followed, is going to change your life forever.

In terms of business let us look at an example of how your frame of mind can influence your future.

Frankie is talking to a friend who has recently been involved in a car accident. As a result, they have issues with getting in and out of the shower in the morning:

- **Old Frankie response**
  - "Yeah, I know, life's a bitch – hey, you'll never guess what happened to me the other day."
- **New Frankie response**
  - "I'm sure there is something we could do together to help with that. Why don't we invent a "getting in the shower" device? We can design it together, I know a chap who invests in such ideas, get it patented and tested then license it to a shower manufacturer".

This may seem farfetched, but your outlook on life can be the difference between spotting opportunities and missing them, totally oblivious to the fact that they ever existed. See the section that refers to Richard Wiseman, The Luck Factor, in part 2 of this book (the chapter called Positive Thinking).

Beliefs come from a lifetime of conditioning and re-enforcement, you need to try to overcome these, and the teachings within this book can help you to achieve this.

Our mind is simply amazing and attempts to re-enforce our beliefs. Whilst this is good in one sense, it can have you believing something for your entire life which is simply incorrect.

We recommend you challenge as many beliefs that you have and seek to justify the belief or disprove it. Think about this – your beliefs may be wrong. A couple of years ago I was speaking with a highly intelligent friend. We were watching a TV program which involved 2 parachutists and one was filming the other. When the chap being filmed pulled the cord, he shot upwards.

My friend stated, "I wonder if that hurts when they go from travelling downwards to all of sudden going upwards". Of course, as he said it, he turned to me with a look of "what have I just said" as he realised that this belief from childhood was indeed incorrect.

Of course, the parachutist did not start going upwards, it just appeared so because they decelerated while the cameraman continued at the same speed.

The point being, our beliefs are immensely powerful and unfortunately, with our brain the way it is, we are very susceptible to what is referred to as confirmation bias, which we touch on later in the book. Therefore, it is important to challenge your own beliefs. If you have a particularly strong political view, for example, try researching, with an **open mind**, an opposing viewpoint; either it will change or reinforce your view, but either way, you have grown because of the exercise.

"Challenge every belief you hold and allow others to challenge your beliefs without blindly defending them – you may just be wrong, and this is how we grow."

We cannot be right all the time and people with very closed minds are exceedingly difficult to communicate with and do not tend to show humility – how does this affect your obituary? You may need to go and re-write it.

Your Last 5 Years

"Your time is limited, so don't waste it living someone else's life"
Steve Jobs

Using the above story of Frankie, go and make yourself a cuppa, download the provided Spreadsheet (The Future You). Now it is time to have a good, hard, honest look at your last 5 years.

How to fill out the spreadsheet.

- Start on the first tab, 'Finance'.

- Complete all the yellow boxes.

  o Add to or change titles but only change the yellow sections.

  o We have not protected it so that you can do with it as you wish.

- Move onto the 'Health Section'.

  o Complete all the yellow sections again.

- Review "The Future You" tab.

What are your thoughts? Disappointed with what you have done over the last 5 years? Ashamed, annoyed with yourself? **WELL, DON'T BE**. This was before you had been introduced to your team. What chance did you have?

Now it would be disappointing if the next 5 years were the same or like the last 5, given the knowledge that you now have.

Perhaps you are happy with how things have been. However, can we improve? Let us aim high. Let us see what we can achieve.

Just look at some of the savings and some of the health improvements you can make. In the current situation that the world faces, isn't it a good time to cut out bad habits and improve our health? Whatever you do, do not be despondent about the position you are in now in any of these areas. You cannot change the past, only influence the future.

"Your living is determined not so much by what life brings to you as by the attitude you bring to life; not so much by what happens to you as by the way our mind looks at what happens." *Khalil Gibran*

It is all about perspective, you cannot change the past – there are only 2 things that you can control:

- Your thoughts.

- Your actions.

Your Fault vs Your Responsibility

While I am a big believer in the notion of, whatever situation you are in, is YOUR RESPONSIBILITY, it is not necessarily your fault but I believe you should ignore the fault aspect. This is worth reading again.

You must distinguish between fault and responsibility. If you blame others for your situation, it will never change because you cannot change others. If, however, you look at a problem as your responsibility to correct and improve, regardless of blame, you begin with a positive attitude towards your situation.

The world today is all about blame; there is a culture that when anything bad happens, someone, or something, must be to blame. So much time and energy is wasted on establishing this, but to what end? It does not change the fact. Forget fault and blame and just take responsibility....for everything in your life.

"If you look at a problem as your responsibility to correct and improve, regardless of blame, you begin with a positive attitude towards your situation."

Why is it not my fault?

Simple, you did not sit there 5 years ago and tell yourself you wanted to be in this negative situation, did you? I am 100% sure you did not. Therefore, you maube did not consciously make the decisions that led to this.

Yes, they were your decisions, but were they made from a perspective of unconsciousness? Did you decide to make these decisions? Of course, you did. However, did you **consciously** think about it before? Did you consult with your team of advisors? No, of course, you did not.

Now, because you know this, this cannot be the case again. For every decision you make, you must check in with the relevant advisor, therefore putting a name and a face/picture, an identity, is very important because they are going to hold you accountable, and you have to answer to them.

Of course, you are answering to yourself and therefore the responsibility is the key to this. Take responsibility for everything in your life, good and bad, and commit to changing them if they need to be changed.

Ashley Kesnar who specialises in alcohol addiction (www.freeyourghost.com) stated on one of her blogs that it is important to "think about the last drink" not the first. The last – and when you have that last drink, are you going to be feeling good? Probably not. This is in keeping with Frankie – ask Frankie now. She also quotes Carl Jung "Until you make the unconscious conscious, it will direct your life and you will call it fate."

Whenever you need to make a decision, "check-in" with Frankie, you, and consider the viewpoints of your 4 advisors. Take note of what each has to say.

Does it all sound a bit weird? Try it and see what you think. Give it a try for just 30 days and see the difference.

Please do not worry about the above – what has happened has happened and it is in the past. The important thing is the future.

What are you going to do differently going forward, based upon the knowledge that you now have?

Your Next Wonderful 5 Years

"Once you choose hope, anything is possible"
Christopher Reeve

Based upon the list that you have created in the previous chapter – what does this future now look like? If you change only one financial and one health aspect, imagine yourself in 5 years. Use the tables later in this chapter to record this information, or in your notebook.

Be aware of 'The Laws of Attraction' and use them to your advantage. There have been several books written and much said around this very topic, and to discuss fully would be beyond the scope of this book. However, simply put, writing down your plans and goals helps to formalise your goals in your mind.

Then picturing the result/s in your mind helps you to visualise your goals, and repeating this process over and over, enables us to achieve our goals with a greater degree of success than otherwise. Simply knowing/believing what is possible enables us to convert these manifestations in our mind into real possibilities.

"If you can see it in your mind, you can hold it in your hand". *Bob Procter*

Visualise your goals. Picture the job/money/house you strive for. Picture the perfect body you command. Imagine the situation you want to achieve. **Picture the fun you will have on the journey**. In each example picture yourself in that situation, with whatever it is you desire.

"Make sure you consider, for these goals, will the journey be happy and enjoyable?"

This last point is so important; if your goals are not going to have an enjoyable journey, are they good goals in the first place?

So, write it down, visualize it, believe it, understand you are worth it and act. Start by writing down your goals/results from the spreadsheet in the following tables, or in your note book:

Financial

E.g. I would have £x more in my bank account

Health

E.g., I could easily run 5km, 10km, Half Marathon, full marathon…..

Morality

E.g., nothing you have done would have negatively
impacted anyone

Legacy

E.g., of all the ideas you have had you have started a
Facebook group that is helping others.

During this process think big. It may not come naturally at first. So, in that event, start small, but remember to re-visit your goals and keep updating them, as your life and goals change. All the time remember to visualize your goals and most important of all, act!

Now imagine that you followed ALL of what you said. Answer these questions:

How much More Money would you have?	
How many steps would you have run/walked?	
How many additional calories have you burnt?	
What could your goal weight be?	
What is your health now, on a scale of 1-10	
What could it be?	
What message would Frankie (the future you) give to you now? E.g., "Stick to it, the rewards far outweigh the hardships"	

Do you like the look of the Future You and how it is shaping up?

We now encourage you to complete "Day One" in the downloads. An example could look like the following:

Which aspects are you going to change?

All of them! I may need help and encouragement on all areas, however, the differences are huge.

I need a full overhaul of my life and now is the time to do it.

What would this mean, based on your findings in the spreadsheet?

I would have saved over £xx !!!!!
I could run 5k/10k or a marathon.
Live longer and more quality time with the kids
Be calmer and more in control of my mind.
HAPPIER !!!!

How am I going to remain focussed?

Reread this book.
Get the mobile app once it is released to track progress
Use the Facebook group for encouragement
Post this on the Facebook page by way of commitment
Do the daily, weekly and monthly check ins.

The Journey to these goals will be pleasurable because?

I will be aware of doing something positive
I will be more connected by living in the present moment
I will be hurting no-one, in fact I will make sure I am helping
people and building a brighter, more positive future for myself and
my family.

3 things I am grateful for.
- This Opportunity to Change
- I have a loving and caring family
- My family and friends are all well
- I have a job, income and a place to live.

SUMMARY

Financi l

Drinking Reduction
Cut out 2 Meals out per
month
Stop the coffee on way
to work

Health

Reduce Alcohol
Improve Sleep
Eat Healthier
Reduce Caffeine

Moral

Stop Speeding
No Mobile whilst
driving
Adopt the daily habits

Legacy

Setup my own business
Actively give back with
volunteering
Donate Blood

Commitment

Name Frankie

Promises:-
- Check in Daily
- Self Observe
- Follow the steps
- Monitor progress
- Have Fun!

Notes:

Think of the achievability of these goals. If you are overwhelmed, consider breaking it down into interim mid-goals. Discuss in your mind with the most relevant advisor, but also consider any implications with other advisors too. Consider how you will achieve each step.

Think of monitoring yourself, by making yourself accountable to one of your advisors, each a role-play advisor or a real-life advisor.

Consider how you might praise/correct yourself. Keep in mind the next step(s) you will take to achieve your goal(s). You could write down these steps, but also make them part of your decision process so they quickly become second nature, and you will subconsciously think of the implications of any actions and will enable you to find the best path to achieve your goals whilst remaining aligned to your overall objectives. Remember putting these ideas down means you are committing to them.

Please feel free to upload your copy to the Facebook Group, this group is private - the community is there to encourage, praise and generally help. You have knowledge that others do not, and the same applies to all members, so collectively we can all assist each other.

To join the Facebook group please visit:
https://www.facebook.com/groups/askfrankiegroup/

This group was made for you – so use it to gain the most benefit.

Within these pages, we will reference material that could help all aspects of your life. Remember, do the right thing, for the right reason and make that decision consciously – always.

Let us be honest, what you have determined as being the changes that you need to make – they are not massive, are they? You are not avoiding people or the things that you enjoy doing. It is just about being sensible.

There is a wealth of informational products out there to help with each aspect and we will refer you to these additional resources throughout and you are free to decide whether to pursue it.

We, the authors read on average, one book on self-help and improvement per month, usually more, and we encourage you to actively increase your knowledge around all areas – it helps to keep your brain active and creative which will give you further ideas.

If you had run for 10 minutes a day for the last 5 years, how different would you be? How about 20 minutes, or even an hour…. visualise and note down what differences would exist.

Do you class yourself as a "slow reader"? I did too, if you want to increase your reading speed by 50 – 100% then we recommend Limitless, by Jim Kwik – a link to this is available in the resources section and our website.

There is also a challenge on Jim Kwiks site that relates to reading 52 books in the next year.

One book per week sounds impossible, or it certainly did to me initially, however it is not. Broken down into manageable chunks while increasing your reading speed and comprehension makes this very achievable.

"Not all readers are leaders, but all leaders are readers."
Harry S. Truman

Knowledge is so powerful and the world we live in today means that you can put this book down now and within seconds you can be reading or watching information on ANY topic. You can learn about anything at all, on-demand.

You should try to use this to your advantage.

Rocket List
You have heard of a bucket list, well let us introduce you to a brand-new term, created by us – **"Rocket List".**

Why not create a reading list, split by topic for all the subject areas that you want to learn?

A Rocket List is a bucket list, but for reading and therefore learning that will 'Skyrocket' your learning and intelligence.

Write the story – Now

"The greatest discovery of my generation is that a human being can alter his life by altering the attitudes of his mind"
William James

How can you write your life story now? Simple - start and visualise it, this serves as a basis on which to manifest the life you want.

Begin now. Make sure you start it in the following way, committing to it, as per the below example, with a date 5 years in advance.

"Today, the xx/xx/20xx, I, Frankie Smith [your name] began a journey 5 years ago to this very day. The steps that I took to change my life in these 5 years were amazingly simple.

Firstly, in the very first year of practising the steps, I was able to
- *X*
- *Y*
- *Z*

I achieved promotion, marathon, financial freedom, health etc...and this was in the very first year.

My goal was for a [car/house/happiness/relationship etc] within the first 5 years. However, the journey that this took me on was very enjoyable. Now, allow me to guide you through all the good things that happened in this period, between 5 years ago and now.

I used to always be anxious, stressed etc. I read the following books.
- *X*
- *Y*

I did the following courses.........."

Have some fun with this – make the goals as huge as you dare and use the daily gratitude that you will start recording later to enrich this story. You really can change anything you want, and to commit it to paper gives you almost a blueprint for the rest of your life, it allows you to enjoy the journey and allows you to do something else which is especially important.

Using it as a diary also allows you to record any events which were not positive, and more importantly, your response to them. As we will discuss in Part 2, most problems are not as big as you think in the grand scheme of life. By addressing these in the way that you can and will, and then recording the solution and the outcome, you can then revisit this and get perspective and the solution to your problem should it re-occur in the future.

Start a new document and begin writing this today – you will be amazed at the results.

Think about what you want your story to be – and think about the obituary you wrote. Success comes in many forms, but for me, it is about doing the right thing and helping as many people as you possibly can. But do this for the right reasons.

Write an overview of the next 5 years, this can be 1 page, or 100+, it is totally up to you. Continue to add to it frequently as this may change day by day.

Regular Review

"All airplanes are off course 99% of the time. The purpose and role
of the pilot and the avionics is to continually bring the plane back
on course so that it arrives on schedule at its destination"

Brian Tracey

Now you have your plan and you have decided what you want to do and what you want to achieve, it is time to run through how you track this. Without regular review, it is impossible to quantify the changes you are making.

Daily, we complete the following and would like to talk through the resources that we have created to assist you now and in the future.

Daily Review
You may decide not to do this daily, and that is fine, do it at whatever frequency that suits you. The aim of this is to act as a planning tool for your day ahead as well as build up a history of daily activity and progress.

I tend to begin completing it at the beginning of the working day and keep it close by for addition and amendment. It never looks particularly neat. Please see below for an example of the Daily Review completed.

This document is yours to complete however you see fit. It is an illustration only but I hope it serves to advise how it could look. Mine end up with scribbles and pictures, even notes from calls.

The downloads hold the template which you are free to copy or amend and make your own.

Again, for accountability, feel free to use the Facebook Group to upload these sheets should you wish.

Plan for Today, goals and targets.
- Shower Meditation
- 10,000 Steps
- Finish Assignment/Business Report
- Read some more of the book I started
- Check in with Myself each time I remember
- Meditation

The Good Points of the Day
Good Run, first in quite a while but I felt great
Got really good praise from my boss at work
My report for work was focussed on environmental improvement

Lessons Learned
Reading really relaxes me. It also takes my mind of other things
and helps me to focus on now

Self-observation makes me realise how much I have achieved in my
life and that the opportunities are endless

What have I achieved today?
Finished the report
Achieved good fitness and Diet
Was the person I view myself to be - stopping to help people or even
just being nice - which is me anyway, but I am now aware of these
actions.

3 things I am grateful for.
- Life
- A job and an income
- A roof over my head

ADVISORS CHECK IN

Financial
No unnecessary
spending

Health
No alcohol

went for a run. Must
Meditate tomorrow

Moral
No actions caused
harm to others

Legacy
My report could make
a difference

Concerns
1 – No meditation

2 – Am I worthy?

3 –

4 –

5 –

Weekly Review

You may or may not have been completing the daily review. However, we stress a weekly review should be carried out for you to ensure you are on the right path.

Again, this is your document, and it can be filled out in any way you like, on the following page is an example of a completed document.

Ensure when you do this that you bear in mind your aims as defined by the spreadsheet and the Five-Year plan in the previous section. How are you progressing? Do you need to realign – could it be worth you reading up on a specific subject for example.

Check-in with your advisors and view yourself as listening to the thoughts from them and taking this in. Does the finance advisor think things are going well? If not, you are not going to be achieving the financial goals, because it is this advisor's job to ensure that you do.

This may feel a little strange at first, but rest assured that it will become second nature quite quickly.

Dive into the key areas and think about what you have done over the last week to drive you towards your goals and targets?

What are you going to do differently between now and next week? Have you noticed an increase in productivity or focus?

If you did not find it beneficial, perhaps you need to be more specific or perhaps it just felt a little silly – please persevere as this really can change your life.

Summary of the Week and Goals Achieved

Week has been great. I estimate that I have saved around £75 above what I would have normally spent. I am fitter and happier.

I have cut out
- *X, Y and Z*

I have started
- *Running, walking and Yoga*

The Good Points

90% of the tasks I set myself I have achieved.
Out of the remaining 10% half are not vital and so I am going to remove them.

I have been praised multiple times at work. I have slept longer and better and as a result I am way more productive.

Lessons Learned

I have the same amount of time as anyone else - not spending all evening in front of the TV/Game console whilst eating and drinking has given me at least 4 hours back, where I have focussed on me.

I can spend hours just reading or reflecting, or going out to see the sunset, or rising early to see the sun rise.

I have wasted so much of my life - but the future will be different.

Goals for Next Week
- *Tick off or remove the 10% from last week*
- *Meditate every day*
- *Continue with the Couch to 5k challenge*
- *Increase step count to 15,000*
- *Continue to feel happy and proud of myself.*

Unfinished Items from Last week
- *Tidy the 'messy draw'*
  - *This is never going to happen, so taking it off :-)*
- *Take all old clothes to the charity shop*
- *Update my CV*

ADVISORS CHECK IN

Financial

You have saved a fortune - why not open a savings account?

Health

No bad habits all week

Health is improving each day

Meditation is helping with your anxiety

Moral

You have completed the Organ donation form and registered to give blood.

Old clothes to charity

Legacy

Volunteer work.

Working on getting my environmental report published

Ideas

1 – Shower Device

2 – Local Business

3 – Write book on X

4 – Dog Walking Business

5- FB Page

Monthly Review

This should be relatively self-explanatory – but in essence, it is your way of keeping track of Frankie for the month that has just passed.

Be detailed and honest here – ultimately, the question is, if you do the same as this each month, are you going to get to where you started in your 5-year plan?

Do not worry if you have strayed off course, recognise it here and be thankful that you have taken the time to do this exercise because (and here is what should be the eye-opener.....)

> *"You have never really realised you were straying off course because you never carried out the exercises in this book. This is how you are where you are and how the future can be so much better!"*

Make sense? You have just identified why plans or aspirations in the past have never come to fruition.

Following is an example of a completed plan.

Summary of the Month and Goals Achieved

Due to stopping X,Y, and Z, I have saved £350 since I started this on the xth of May 2020

I can now run for 2k quite easily.

Getting great praise at work, almost daily - I feel like it was always there, I just had an extremely negative view on it.

I have also read 2 books....2!!!!!

The Good Points

My report has been put forward for innovation award.
Fitness and finance is better today than last month.

Friends have commented about me being more fun to be around, looking fitter and happier.

I had a random chat with a stranger in the local shop and turns out she knows my boss - who agreed with the praise she gave!!!

Lessons Learned

It is better to trust first until someone gives me a reason not to.

I am so much more productive and sleeping better due to
-   X
-   Y
-   Z

I have all the time in the world to do what I want and I can be Happy!!!

Goals for Next Month

Increase again in steps
Get to 5k running
Continue to follow the advice in the book.
Stop doing
-   X,Y,Z
Continue doing
-   A,B,C
Start Doing
-   D,E and F

Unfinished Items from Last Month

Still not doing daily meditation, yet I know it really helps me.

3 items remain on my todo list.

ADVISORS CHECK IN

Financial

Awesome Job!!!.
Savings huge.

GO TREAT YOURSELF!

Health

Buzzing!!! No complaints but please do the meditation

Moral

All actions are pure.

Well done and keep going.

Legacy

You have saved a fortune - why not open a savings account

Best Ideas of each week

1 – Dog Walking Business

2 –

3 –

4 –

Annual Review

You will now be at the 1/5 point and time to assess your progress.
Use this sheet to record as much as you can.
Review each of the monthly updates in this session and take as
much time as you need. A useful exercise here is to also complete
the spreadsheet again and see how this differs.

If you are not on track for the goals that you laid out, why not?
Perhaps the answer to this is that your goals have changed which is
also fine. Everything is fine and it is happening just as it should.

Review the months, assess against where you expected to be at this
stage and then make the tweaks and go forwards. Do not regret
anything, just make the changes that are needed and carry on.

Let's face it, if even one of the elements in the original plan is on
track, you are in a far better position than you were when you
started the journey.

Then make the necessary adjustments to get yourself back on track.
Do not be too hard on yourself if you have strayed off course, just
gently bring yourself back.

Summary of the Year and Goals Achieved

What a Year. I estimate I have saved over £10,000 and have drastically improved my health.

I have reduced my weight by 10% and I can run for hours if I needed to.

I have been praised at work for positivity and as a result I got a promotion without even trying

I am also a lot more in control of my emotions and my anxiety levels have seriously dropped.

The Good Points

Report put forward for the Innovation of the year award.

Lots of comments about my positivity both at work and at home. Due to a reduction in alcohol, I enjoy the social occasions so much more due to it being a treat rather than the norm.

I tried mountain climbing for the first time and I have the bug.

Lessons Learned

Take control of yourself rather than letting life pass you by. Write down the goals and see how they come to life.

I have regular 'chats' with my advisors ahead of major decisions - I haven't impulse bought for months.

You attract what you think of - think negative and you attract negatives - remain positive and be grateful for what you have.

Goals for Next Year

London Marathon

Start a side business

Make the £10k savings work for me, possibly invest in a small local business that needs help in this difficult time.

Offer my expertise in my field to others via the LinkedIn advisor status.

Manifest the actions of the environmental report and change the world for the better.

Unfinished Items from Last Year

Complete a course on NLP/CBT

Register as advisor on LinkedIn.

Push a talent over Fiverr.com to assist others and earn extra money

ADVISORS CHECK IN

Financial

Awesome . No other word for it. Well done and again, treat yourself.

Health

Wow - just Wow. 10% lighter, 100% fitter and mental health is much improved.

Just remember the meditation.

Moral

Lots of volunteering and blood donations.

All actions have helped and not harmed others

Legacy

Your paper is being acted upon.

You have the opportunity to drive the changes and forever change the environment. Well done.

Top Ideas to Pursue

1 – Dog walking business

2 – etc

3 – etc

4 – etc

5- etc

Part 2 – Be the Best That You Can Be

Be the Best Version of you

"It doesn't matter where you are coming from. All that matters is where you are going"
Brian Tracy

Before you go any further – watch the following video.
https://bit.ly/3zxRQ89
Do feel better about who you are and what you have? Even just a little bit?

Now that you have assessed where you are and where you are going, I truly hope that you have real excitement about the future – you can, after all, do anything that you set your mind to.

This second half of the book is all-around key areas that can assist you going forward. They are a collection of our thoughts and suggestions – practical advice that we have used throughout our careers and lives in general.

Please view these in the way they are intended – not instructions but suggestions which you may wish to adapt to suit some ideas of your own – they have helped us and so maybe they can help you too.

You will find reference to other texts in the following sections, all of which are recommended reading. It is worth re-reading your own story and your obituary before proceeding. The best version of you is purely based upon that. This is quite subjective, and you need to know what you want your message to be.

We cover several different areas, and it is important to note that they are not instructions, but advice that you may decide to adopt, or not.

The important thing is to decide, today, what you want your life to be about and take decisive action to start that journey.

One of the most important aspects for us is positive thinking. This has been discussed a lot of times, by a lot of people, but I think it is important to discover what it is and the difference it can make. The first chapter in this section is around just that.

As we mention, one of the most useful tools that you have is the *inability* to think of 2 things at the same time. Therefore, if you are thinking positively, you cannot be thinking negatively.

Try to replace as much negativity with positivity because that attracts further positivity. If you do nothing else in the review documents, try to start noting down what you are grateful for each day.

If you cannot think of anything you are grateful for then I have some amazing news. We all have something we should be grateful for and if you don't believe that, I would argue that you are not looking hard enough. The great news is that once you start to look and identify positives, you will begin to notice and attract more of that into your life. Start now!

Positive thinking

"Whether you think you can, or think you can't, you are right".
Henry Ford

In other words, you become your thoughts and you must recognise this and ensure that those thoughts are positive, the difference is simply life-changing. By this, we do not mean imagine that you are a Premier League footballer and tomorrow you find yourself pulling up to training in a Ferrari.

However, on this same strand, thinking you could **never** achieve this is guaranteeing that you will not. So instead, start with a positive mindset. Try turning negatives into positives.

For example, try to replace sentences, such as those below.

Replace this	With this
"I wish I wasn't Overweight"	"I will get to my goal weight"
"I wish I wasn't skint"	"I have money to survive, and I would love to be financially independent"
"I hate my Job"	"I am going to get a Job that I prefer or change my career"

Use this skill in your language and conversation. It will soon become second nature, and you may be surprised by the results.

"The mind is like Velcro for negative experiences, and Teflon for positive ones." *Rick Hanson...and my Mum*

Become aware of how you speak and think and every time you hear a negative – recognise it and change it for the future. Your brain does not recognise words such as "Don't" when in a sentence.

Disagree? Let me tell you this.....
Don't think of a red car.

What did you think of?

Or perhaps a more modern example - have you ever searched on google for something but excluding something else? Go to google and search for the following:

"Show me a picture of a car that is not red" or "Show me a picture of any colour car but not red".

What images are you presented with? It is almost as if you are saying (or searching for) "think of a red car". The structure of your language is therefore especially important – especially your internal language to yourself.

We, the authors, are positive people, and we can tell you that negativity is very apparent in others and therefore can have a huge impact on your interaction with them.

Some further examples to change into everyday language would be:

Instead of these	Try these
- Don't do that	- Do this
- I hate that	- I prefer this
- She is terrible	- Her behaviour could be more desirable
- That's awful	- That could be better.

Negative Thoughts

Please read the following and read it very carefully.

"The average person has 60,000 thoughts per day. Of those thoughts: 95 percent repeat each day, and, on average, 80 percent of repeated thoughts are negative." *The Cleveland Clinic*

Does that blow your mind as much as it does ours? This equates to 45,600 negative and repetitive thoughts and the main problem with this is the fact of repetition.

When you have a negative thought and allow it to pass, there is no real issue. However, dwelling on that thought and, as the statistic before shows, reliving this same thought over and over repeatedly is simply magnifying and intensifying the feelings that these thoughts bring.

We have said *"when"* we have a negative thought because we all have thoughts that we are largely not in control of – when standing at the top of a large building, we may have the thought "what if I jumped?". Well, it would hurt – a lot – and you would probably die, therefore you don't do it. The point is if you have these thoughts, do not think that you are in some way different; we all have them, it's how you react to them that makes the difference.

You can change your thoughts and it is as simple as recognising the negatives and replacing them with the positives. We cannot hold 2 thoughts in our minds at the same time which is a real positive in this case.

If something is bothering you, a common piece of advice is to "don't think about it". Now, whilst this is well-intended, you are being told NOT to think about something but, in order not to think about it – you must first think about it to make sure you are not thinking about it. Think about that last sentence for a spell, (remember the red car example above?).

"If you are overwhelmed by a thought – think about something else – create that 'Happy Thought' which could be anything that makes you smile – and have that on hand to think about whenever you need to."

In other words, build a tool to combat negative or low moods, by having a thought that you can recall to mind. For me, this is sitting at the viewpoint of Surprise View in the Lake District. I go there regularly both physically and in my mind when I need to. Videos can be viewed here:

https://www.facebook.com/thefutureyou1 or
https://bit.ly/3gJhUV6

Build a whole "fantasy" around this if it helps, add people and situations or whatever is needed to help you to feel good. Then, when the need arises, think of that.

I love this quote:

"I have been through some terrible things in my life, some of which actually happened." *Mark Twain*

It is a great quote that sums up the fact that most situations that happen in our lives to increase our stress and anxiety, happen only in our minds.

What is the worst that could happen?
For every issue that arises, try the following. Ask yourself the following questions:
- What is the worst that can happen?
- What is the best that can happen?
- What is in the middle of these two and therefore the most likely?

So, as an example, you need to give a speech at a family event.
What is the worst that could happen?
- I could forget all my words.
- Everyone will laugh at me.
- I could offend people.
- I will spoil the whole party.
What is the best that could happen?

- I remember all my words.
- The audience loves it and laughs throughout.
- I receive praise from all the guests.
- I get selected for a TV show (yeah, ok, perhaps a little optimistic but you get the point).

What is the Middle ground and therefore most likely?
- I will forget a couple of words.
- Get through it unscathed.
- Receive praise and get a lot of laughs.
- Everyone wants you to do well – you will.

The point is that things are rarely as bad as they first seem and keeping a hold of that thought can greatly reduce your anxiety and stress both in general and in that situation.

Things are rarely as bad as they first seem.
This is a true statement – think of any issue that you have had over the last year – when it first came to light it seemed huge and insurmountable until your amazing brain kicked in to solve the problem for you or help you to deal with it. Of course, some occurrences such as bereavement for example are, but we are talking more generally, on average, over a period of time. However, even with the worst that has happened, have you managed? Did you cope better than you *thought* you would? Again, thought is the issue once again.

And how do you feel about it now that it is over? Was it anywhere near as bad as you thought? Of course, there may well be examples where it was, but I am talking about "on average"; in most cases, it was not as bad as you first thought.

Even if it was, did you handle it better than you thought? Is it not the case that the thought of something is often far worse than the actual event?

About bereavement, my worst fear of suddenly dying is the thought of how my loved ones would react. The thought of them sad, upset and devastated would be worse for me than dying. On that basis, how would your lost loved one feel about your upset? If they could speak to you now, what would they say? Would they want you to be sad? Or would they want you to be happy and live the best life you can? That is not to say that you should not be sad about the loss, but when you start to feel happier, do not feel guilty for that.

They will always exist in your heart. Do you not agree? What would you want to say to the people you left behind if this was you? Picture the scene after your passing – how would you want them to feel?

Our minds are conditioned by the past and it is easy to reside in a place that breeds negativity. On the whole, there is no such thing as someone just being unlucky or living a life where everything that happens to them is bad. This is a perception they hold and unfortunately it then often manifests the results.

You get more of what you think about; think bad things will happen and they seem to, why? Because that person is looking for proof to justify that.

"I never win anything".

Yeah, who does? I do not think I have ever won anything, the odd small win on the lottery, but not a car, or a holiday etc. Does this make me unlucky? Well, yes actually, if I start to think about it and mull it over and believe it. However, I do not, because I am not; most people do not win the lottery or the holiday/car on some TV show. But it is that thought process around that which gives rise to your opinion.

Self-Fulfilling Prophecies
This can be extremely dangerous and tends to centre around negative thoughts and acting on them. To describe this better I

would like to tell you a story that my Dad told me once about 2 farmers.

Old Macdonald had a farm….and it was time for harvest, however, he has a problem. His Combine Harvester is broken. So, what can he do?

Well, Farmer Giles, his neighbour, has one and maybe he could borrow that. So, he sets off walking to ask that exact question. On the journey, he talks to himself:

"last time I borrowed it, I took it back late, I damaged the paintwork which I had promised to get repaired, but I have forgotten about that until now. He probably needs it at this time of year and maybe won't be prepared to share."

So, when Old Macdonald got to Farmer Giles' door, he knocked, and the door was opened by a very friendly and jolly farmer. Old Macdonald said, "forget it", and walked off.

In other words, he had convinced himself so much that the other farmer would not lend it to him that he had not even bothered to ask.

This is quite an exaggerated story, but it goes to prove a point – do not pre-empt how someone else will be and do not allow your happiness to be based on their actions.

Turn that around and think about the story again where he spends the journey thinking of all the positives and all the reasons why a person would, and you have a completely different outcome.

How many times have you gone for a job interview for example, for a job that you could easily do, and you have been rather indifferent; "if I get it cool, if not then I am happy where I am". I bet you got offered the job.

Conversely, have there been interviews that you have gone for where the job would be awesome, it would change your life and then, at that time, that is all that mattered – I bet you did not get offered the job.

Why is this? We believe that it is simply the fact that when you are relaxed and calm about something, your true self begins to shine through, and you do not try too hard. For the latter job, you may also have had niggling doubts about whether you deserved that job, and this comes through. Be yourself, be authentic, what will be will be and be amazed at the outcome

Positivity breeds positivity. You get what you focus mostly on in life. If you focus on the lack of something and what you do not have, such as you don't have a nice car, a big house or a high-powered job, then you attract more of that lack into your life.

However, if you adopt the "attitude of gratitude" - being grateful for everything you have (as per the video at the beginning of this chapter, you are better off than a significant proportion of the world), that must be something that you are grateful for.

Focusing on what you have brings more of it. It also puts you out there with a far more positive attitude which means you meet people, and they like to be around you. That could present job, business or personal development opportunities. Whereas a negative approach creates a feeling of lack, a feeling of "why me" and people do not enjoy being around that negativity.

"At the end of the day, people won't remember what you said or did, they will remember how you made them feel", *Maya Angelou*
This is an important point because again, it is thought (in this case the other persons thought) that determines their image of you.

Think about this for a second – every person you ever meet has a different opinion of who you are and what you are all about. Whilst you can influence this to a certain extent, you cannot change other people's perception 100% of the time, just always be the best that you can be.

However, always try to give a reflection of the true you out into the universe and people will see that. Be honest and be yourself; it is easier and far more enjoyable.

Filtering and Confirmation Bias

Your brain is breath-taking in its abilities – there are numerous facts I could list around this but to give you an example, your subconscious is constantly filtering.

Filtering
Filtering is where mundane and irrelevant information is constantly being filtered out without you ever being aware of it. For example, when was the last time you saw a specific type of car, say a blue car of a certain brand? You will probably struggle to remember this information.

However, if you have decided to buy a blue car of your chosen brand you will notice everyone that passes you. (There is also a good chance that you will notice one today having read this. Ask your brain to point one out to you right now and see what happens over the course of the day.)

Whilst filtering is vital to your sanity, (you receive so much information every second and if your brain did not filter this out you would be overwhelmed within seconds), it also means you miss a lot in your daily life. This is where stopping and taking a moment to observe yourself is especially important. Doing this is simple – observe yourself from outside yourself.

In the book "The Volunteer", a true story about a resistance hero who Infiltrated Auschwitz during the war, there are details of how the main character, Witold Pilecki, carried out this exact exercise. He would imagine himself outside of his body, observing himself and the horrendous, squalid and horrifying environment in which he found himself seemed not to be quite so bad when viewed from the 3rd person. More on this later.....

Confirmation Bias
Confirmation Bias is also worthy of mention and it is a reason why your beliefs are made so strong. In brief, this is where you have a belief and your subconscious constantly finds ways to back that up.

This could be any belief that you have and the difficulty in identifying those beliefs and challenging them. An example of confirmation bias is as follows.

You believe that the education system in this country is appalling for one reason or another, built up over time. You are reading the newspaper one morning and on page 11 there is an article advising that exam results dropped by 5% in the latest GCSE and A-Level results – you skim the article and that is your takeaway, you do not analyse the 5% and what it means.

You read but ignore/dismiss completely the write up on page 2 about the steady increase in the difficulty of the exams and how any drop in results should be viewed in this context. The article explains that they are harder by 10%, but again, the 2 stories are not considered in conjunction with each other, even though this was more prominent, on a page closer to the front page.

In other words, you are seeking out information that confirms your currently held opinion, while passing over those that do not agree with your preconceived notions, even considering new evidence, and all of this without you knowing it.

Recent times have made this even more difficult to break free from; social media is intelligent enough to recognise your bias and then curate the content that you see so that it is consistent with your beliefs. How often does YouTube or other social media give you recommendations of specific content and recommendations across different platforms?

We all do this and are completely unaware of it – again being aware of this is especially important as knowledge is power and if you understand this, you can begin to challenge your beliefs or allow others to, with humility and therefore you can grow. How can you be 100% sure that you are right in your opinion if you have not first considered the opposing view and researched it? If you haven't, you are blindly believing the viewpoint.

Try this for the next 28 days, observe your surroundings as often as you can – if you are travelling in a car, notice the makes, models and colours of the cars that you are passing. Try looking for one that is the same as your own, or the one that you are thinking of buying. Similarly, if you have some extraordinarily strong opinions about something, try to seek out and read the opposing view and listen to counter-arguments to your beliefs – this is not admitting you are wrong, but rather proving your open-mindedness.

Also, try not to mindlessly watch content that is put in front of you, rather seek out opposing viewpoints as mentioned earlier, but harness the power of social media, the more diverse you can be, the more diverse content you will receive.

Perhaps a conflicting viewpoint here is to take time away from any social media content – switch it off and enjoy the 'boredom'.

Too Positive?

I have, in the past, been pulled up on the fact that not everything can be great. And by this, I mean, it is not uncommon for me to say a meal is the best I have had, or a holiday is the best holiday ever! It is very common.

That is how I shape my outlook; I like to think of everything in a positive aspect. Imagine this, think about:
- Your house
- Your car
- Your last holiday

Now, if I ask you to name your **dream**:
- House
- Car
- Holiday

I am sure the 2 lists won't be the same. Why? Because as we have said we are always striving for bigger and better and the journey is not where you see happiness, but instead the end goal.

Take someone who owns a BMW, their dream car is probably a Ferrari. Whereas someone who owns an old car may have the dream of that BMW. How many people have you heard of that own their dream anything? Or do they say, "it's nice, but we could do with an extra bedroom, greater horsepower"....you get the point.

Imagine if you can get to the point, like the Stoic philosophy, where "what you *really want*, is what you *actually have*". In other words, your car is your dream car as is your house etc. Live in this belief and watch your happiness and contentedness improve.

That is not to say that you should not aim high and those aims may well be bigger and better, but the point is to be content with what you have now.

Make a list of the things you cherish most in your life and what brings you the most happiness. This could time with your friends and family, walking in the countryside. List 5 things in this category. If the 5 things you noted down, you currently have (such as your family, kids) then you are off to a great start.

Some people believe that they would be happy if they won the lottery, but how many millionaires are not happy? Winning the lottery can cause certain stresses such as:
- Who do you give to?
- Who are my real friends?
- Can any friends made after a win be real?

It can cause stress and anxiety. Lovemoney.com states that **"Believe it or not, statistics show 70% of lottery winners end up broke and a third go on to declare bankruptcy".**

Material possessions, both present and in the future, cannot make you happy in the long term so be grateful for what you have right here, right now. Don't believe me? Then think about the following.

What is the most expensive, item you have bought apart from your home? This could be a car or any other material item. How happy did you feel when you collected it? How happy did you feel the month following? How do you feel about it now? Remember to consider everything, such as the cost of upkeep etc.

Uplifting Content
We feel incredibly honoured that Ione wrote our foreword, her ethos is so well aligned to ours in many ways. One thing that is so important in positive thinking is to give yourself a good supply of good news.

Every day I read at least one story from "Uplifting Stories" a book written by Ione; they do make you feel good. Try to build this into your life too.

I love this short story that I heard years ago, from where I can't remember:

There was a ferry taking people from one island to another, where they were to live forever.

Passenger 'A' spoke to the captain and asked what were the people like on the island they were going to? "What are they like where you came from?" asked the captain.

"They were self-centred, unkind and nasty" replied passenger 'A'. The captain looked sad and said "I'm afraid you will find them the same on this island"

A little later, passenger 'B' spoke to the captain and asked what were the people like on the island they were going to? "What are they like where you came from?" asked the captain.

"They were lovely, so kind and friendly – I am going to miss them" replied passenger 'B' warmly. The captain smiled and replied "I think you will find them the same on this island"

You must try to maintain a positive outlook. As the saying goes:
"Everything will be okay in the end. If it's not okay, it is not the end.", *John Lennon*

Try to recognise your negative thoughts and replace them with positives. Check in with yourself regularly and have the humility to challenge all the thoughts you hold. You cannot think of 2 things at the same time so if a thought is troubling you, force yourself to think about something else – your happy thought.... a family holiday, a secluded beach – anything that makes you stop thinking about what is stressing you. Being aware of this has already begun to reduce the power of your negative thoughts.

Richard Wiseman, in his book "The Luck Factor", studies the most and least lucky people. What is interesting is that the lucky class themselves as lucky and the opposite is also true. This is a fascinating assessment of what constitutes luck and I highly recommend it.

I think it highlights the fact that people can manifest and create self-fulfilling prophecies based upon their outlook on life. The studies show, via experiment, that those who class themselves as lucky have a greater ability to spot opportunities. In one example, this included a 'lucky' man noticing money on the floor and an 'unlucky' woman missing it.

If you think you are unlucky, read the following from Richards book. Is this bad luck or a pure and simple coincidence?

"In June 1980, Maureen Wilcox bought tickets for both the Massachusetts lottery and the Rhode Island Lottery. Incredibly, she managed to choose the winning numbers for both lotteries but didn't win a penny — her Massachusetts numbers won the Rhode Island lottery and her Rhode Island numbers won the Massachusetts lottery."

Is this bad luck? Well it all depends how you choose to look at it; undoubtedly this is a devastating occurrence, one that would leave you feeling very disappointed. However, in my opinion, it is nothing more than a coincidence; a very remote and highly unlikely coincidence, but a coincidence nonetheless.

Focus on yourself only
Allow me to ask you a question, which would you prefer?
1. Would you rather earn 50,000 a year while others make 25,000 OR
2. Would you rather earn 100,000 a year while others make 250,000

*Currency symbols removed and assuming everything costs the same in both scenarios.

Amazingly, in a study by the LA Times in 2008, the majority of people asked would choose option 1. They would prefer to earn half the amount, providing it was double that of their friends and peers.

How can this be? Again, it is down to perception and that very dangerous practice of comparing yourself to others which, as we will explore later, is at a huge detriment to your happiness.

Your Amazing Brain
Lastly, on this subject, I would like to refer to the work of someone that I hold in extremely high regard, Derren Brown.   Having attended most of his live shows and watched all his TV shows, I find him fascinating.

His "Bootcamp for the Brain" series on Audible is truly fascinating, covering topics around luck, randomness and how understanding your mind and its 'quirkiness' can assist you in harnessing its power to greatly improve your life.

Something that I have mentioned throughout this book is that you cannot focus on 2 things simultaneously and Derren covers this in true, magical style, with a couple of experiments, one of which requires you to think of   4 letter word which.....well, go and listen to it – that will put a lot of this into context.

Anxiety, Worry and Happiness

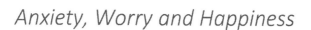

"Too many of us are not living our dreams because we are living our fears" Les Brown

Observe Your Thoughts

We believe we are the only species that can do this. When you are observing your thoughts, you are Frankie in the present. Become Frankie, and when you have negative or overwhelming thoughts just be aware of them – if they are about stressful situations, become aware of what you are thinking and observe them as Frankie – you will be amazed at how less stressful that situation will become.

Sometimes it can help to move out of yourself and view yourself from behind. Look at the person that is you and think "they are worried about X,Y,Z, it isn't so important in the grand scheme of things." Taking this time to watch yourself dealing with worry, removes a lot of the 1st person from the situation and a lot of the power, as described in the last chapter concerning Auschwitz.

If you ever feel overwhelmed, check out the following links.

Most Relaxing Video Ever
(https://bit.ly/3i1IBXd)

Perspective
(https://bit.ly/3c0dp77)

In his audiobook, Power of Now, Craig Beck talks about the moment of now. That moment is all you have – the past and the future do not exist – living in the now moment is hugely important to your happiness and wellbeing, I strongly urge you as part of this process to actively read such books – this is one that I would highly recommend. You can find links to recommended reading in the references section and at www.ask-frankie.com.

Anxiety is a big problem and a lot of what we worry about is in our mind. What if you were told that a child had been killed in a road accident - the actual occurrence has not caused any upset to you, but it is your knowledge and subsequent thoughts around it that does. Don't agree? Well, now imagine you are told that the story was made up; your upset was real, but the event never actually happened....it wasn't the event, it was your thoughts around it.

If you never find out about that incident you could never be upset about it, so it cannot be the incident in isolation that has caused your pain.   Now that is not to say that you should get to a point where you aren't upset or affected by such horrendous things.

The point is that it is not the incident, but your reaction and thoughts around it that gives it emotional power. If somebody says something bad to you at work, different people will react in different ways. Some people just push it away and not think about it.   For some people, it will not even register on their radar as being a problem yet other people will dwell on it.

Humans are the only species that will replay a bad situation rather than forget it. Remember the statistic earlier about negative thoughts? In case you missed it, here it is again.

"The average person has 60,000 thoughts per day. Of those thoughts: 95 percent repeat each day, and, on average, 80 percent of repeated thoughts are negative." The Cleveland Clinic

Take an animal that has had its home destroyed - it does not sit there and think "why did this happen to me", "this is so unfair", "someone needs to help me out" no, they just rebuild the home and carry on.

Or a Gazelle being chased by a lion – when the Gazelle escapes, the Gazelle goes straight back to grazing – it appears unfazed by the horrendous near-death experience. The moment has passed, and the animal is continuing to live in the present. They do not go and find the first friend they can and tell them how bad the experience was, or post on social media about the horrific experience (and probably how they handled it so well).

The wildlife scenario is not strictly applicable to humans; however, we do dwell on things; something will be said at work and you may replay that conversation over and over and think about it constantly, well into the night, therefore disrupting sleep patterns and making the cycle worse.

Frankie, or the future you, can be greatly beneficial in this sense because if you find yourself anxious or worried about something, come out of your body and observe yourself - observe the fact that you are worried about this 'thing'.

What this does is have a dramatic and profound shift in power and focus because you are observing yourself worrying – that worry has just lost a large proportion of its power – why? Because you are viewing the worry as the 3rd person.

How many times have friends shared problems with you and you thought **"I would switch my problems with you in a heartbeat"** - does that mean their problem is insignificant? No, but it means when you are out of the situation, they do not seem so big - you feel better about the problem. Try it, it works.

Think for a second about an anxious situation you experienced in the last year. Remember how you felt and then compare that to how you think of that same situation now that it has passed. This is like viewing as the 3rd person and therefore demonstrates the power of that technique.

Another enormously powerful method to cope with anxiety is to look at how things could be so much worse. In other words, if you have something that is worrying you currently, be it financial, health or anything else, do this:
- Close your eyes.
- Imagine your worst nightmare!
  - This could be anything.

- o E.g., being stuck in a foreign prison, in fear of your life.
- Whatever the nightmare is, it must be horrendous - make it as bad and as dark as you like – no one is going to know what you are thinking of.
- Live it – see the sights, in colour in your mind.
- Imagine any smells that may be associated with it.
- Make it big and bright, colourful, and loud – imagine the sounds.
- Live this for 5 minutes
  - o What are people doing or saying to you in this environment.
  - o Are you close to serious injury or even death?
- **STOP.**
- Open your eyes – think about your current situation – is it that bad?

Do this whenever you feel down. I can promise you one thing, there will be someone in a worse situation than you are currently in – regardless of your situation. It will be nowhere near as bad as what some people have gone or are going through - the most horrendous atrocities, personal loss or living every day in poverty - living every day without fresh water or the constant fear of their life. How can I be sure that someone is worse off? Because you are reading this; some don't have even the small luxury of being able to read or being able to afford the cost of a book.

I can guarantee that **my** problems are worse than **yours**. I can also guarantee **your** problems are worse than **mine**. Sounds contradictory? The point is, my problems are worse than yours – **to me.** And yours are worse than mine, **to you.** It is all about perspective and moving to more of a 3rd person view of your life can help enormously.

We are all going to die.
No matter who you are, in 100 years you are not going to be here anymore. In a further 100 years, nobody is going to care about you at all unless you do something massive to change the world.

This may sound like something that should make you anxious, rather than alleviate it but think about this. You can spend the rest of your life worrying about, for example, dying or falling ill, only for it to happen.

When it happens, do you think to yourself, "I knew that would happen, and I was right all the time, I'm happy now" or "I wish that I had just enjoyed these past years"?

Death is inevitable and it should be used as a tool to encourage you to get up and do your best in every way, every day. As said in part 1 of the book – write your obituary.

Look at this – these are the top 10 regrets that dying people have – perhaps this can act as a rule book to live by.
https://www.powerofpositivity.com/life-regrets-people/

1. "I wish I had Lived for myself more".
2. "I wish I hadn't worked so hard".
3. "I wish I didn't hold back my feelings".
4. "I wish I had stayed in touch".
5. "I wish I was happier".
6. "I wish I cared less of what other people think".
7. "I wish I didn't worry so much".
8. "I wish I had taken better care of myself".
9. "I wish I didn't take life for granted".
10. "I wish I lived in the now"

There is Power in Insignificance
In his bestselling book, Life in Half a Second, Matthew Michealewicz
states:

"Planet Earth is four-and-a-half billion years old. The species you and I
belong to, Homo sapiens, did not emerge until some 200,000 years ago.
The oldest known fossils of modern humans are only 160,000 years old,
discovered in Herto, Ethiopia. So out of the four-and-a-half billion years
that this planet has been floating through the nothingness of space,
we've been around some .0044% of that time. Put another way, if our
planet was exactly one year old, then modern humans would have only
been around for the last 23 minutes. Measured on the same scale, if our
planet was a year old, then your entire life would amount to half a
second."

This creates a feeling of insignificance but can also have a profound
effect.

Anxiety and worry can come about from a feeling of
underachievement and that your life should be about something
more. However, when you read the above fact and also think about
the following statistic:

**"There are more stars in our universe than there are grains of sand
on the Earths beaches",** *Carl Sagan*

You begin to realise that we belong to something so vast, that we
largely *are* insignificant to the universe, and yet we are vital to its
continuation – everything in the universe is just right for life, and
for us to exist, including our existence. This, I find, takes a little of
the pressure off.

You are simply amazing; you were born against all the odds and you
are living a life that is worth living; think about what you have
achieved:
- You could communicate through speech, probably, by the
  time that you were 1-2 years of age!

- You can read these words – an extraordinarily complex language, but you have nailed it.
- Countless other things, that take huge amounts of cognitive effort and co-ordination – walking and driving to name only two.

You are amazing and you can achieve yet more amazing things if you allow yourself to. Do not believe me?

Take Alex Flynn as an example. You can read more about Alex at the following website: (www.alexflynn.co.uk/). Alex who, at the age of 36 was diagnosed with Parkinson's disease, decided to travel 1 million steps to prove it was not going to keep him down. Having smashed that by 2015, he now got his sights set to be the first person with Parkinson's disease to climb to the summit of Mount Everest in 2022.

My attempt to point out the insignificance is not to reduce the worthiness of life, quite the opposite; you have been given something so precious that you should/could make the most of it.

By being aware of this, the pressure on you should be greatly reduced – there is nothing that you cannot achieve if you put your mind to it.

In her highly inspirational book, "Rebel's Guide to Spirituality", Ania Halama refers to a quote that both proves the enormity of the university, but also your role in it.

"You are not a drop in the ocean; you are the entire ocean in a drop" *Rumi*

A lot has been written around this topic and consider some of the following.
- You could not exist without the universe.
- Animals could not exist without plants.

- The Earth could not exist without EVERYTHING that is currently in the universe.

Therefore, whilst the comment above is true "You could not exist without the Universe", is it not also true that the universe could not exist without you, right now?

You are important, valuable, and vital to the world, try not to forget that. When you consider all of the variables required for the universe and you to exist, it's a miracle that you are here at all – you must have superpowers. The question is, what are you going to with them?

"You are a ghost driving a meat covered skeleton made from stardust riding a rock floating through space. Fear Nothing",
Whisper

Nothing Stays the Same
This should **Blow Your Mind!** – every time you shuffle a deck of cards, it is likely you are the first person **EVER** to have put the cards into that exact sequence, why? Because there are 8 x 10^{67} combinations; "**more ways to shuffle a deck than there are atoms on earth.**" (buzzfeed.com).

Watch a river, look at the river today and tomorrow and it may look the same as it did yesterday but it's not - that water particles make-up is not the same as it was yesterday or even a second ago – some (albeit minuscule) erosion has also taken place.

"You cannot step into the same river twice",
Heraclitus

It may look the same, but it's different – every second of every day the world is in a position that it will never be in again, or ever has been previously. At the time of writing, the following is true, as published by livepopulation.com

- Total Population – 7.6 Billion
- Births today – 179k
- Deaths today – 75k

Also, consider this, there is a notion that due to the cells in our body dying and being replaced constantly, that every 7 years we are completely different people in every sense, every cell has been replaced. Sadly, upon research it appears this is not 100% correct in its entirety, however, due to cells being replaced, we are not the *exact* person we were, second by second.

What's the Problem?
You probably feel like you have new problems every day and if this were the case, then please try this exercise.
- Think back over the last 5 years.
- Write down every problem or worry that caused you stress and anxiety.

By rights, if you had a new problem or worry every day you should now be sat with a list of 1,825 – I reckon your list is not that long. Why? Simply because what you view as a problem today will be forgotten very quickly once it is sorted – and because, like the river, everything constantly changes, problems will get solved and worries will disappear – just let them flow like the river.

You may say, "how on earth can you expect me to remember every single problem over 5 years?". When the problem occurred, did you ever think that you would simply forget it? No, because there and then, it was a problem – you thought about it and mulled it over in your mind. Once sorted, they simply disappear, forgotten; imagine the difference in your life if you can adopt the 3rd person view of that problem at the time, much like you are doing now.

Now, from your list, do the following calculation (assuming your list contained 50 problems.

- 1825 (no of days) **Divided by** the No. of problems = x
- E.g., 1825/50 = 36.5

Therefore, you can expect a problem, that is noteworthy (because that is all the problems you can remember) every 36 days. That's not so bad, is it? Now forget that and get on with your life – don't look for problems.

Your Happiness and Other People
Do not let your happiness be dependent on other people's actions, you cannot control them, nor should you try. You may do something good for someone and they may not thank you in the way that you would have thanked them. For example, you may have bought them a gift or a card and yet they haven't done anything for you, just said thanks.

Does this mean they are wrong, and you are right? No, just you are both different people. If you allow that to be a reason to upset you and you, therefore, continue to play that round and round and round in your mind it becomes a big issue, and your happiness is therefore **ALWAYS** based on other people's actions.

"There are only 2 things that YOU can control. Your thoughts and your actions. That's all. Control them wisely."

Other people's actions could be the result of their current situation and we have no idea what is going on in their lives. Someone may be rude to you in a supermarket or other setting which could affect your mood but what issues do they have going on in their lives? Try to ignore this and carry on without playing it over and over, instead, think of your happy thought. Perhaps a kind word to that person and a smile may make the difference to them.

"A situation only has power if you give it thought".

Try to avoid reading too much into social media, I would go so far as to say sometimes it is good to take a break from it altogether. Our feeds are filled with the absolute best, and in some cases, the fabricated reality that some people are living. Other media, such as TV does not help this either.

Take for example a film about Christmas, with the huge house, perfect decorations, and perfectly cooked turkey, served at the table fit for Royalty. Where are the "emergency chairs"? Where are the people sitting at a table, with different sized chairs, or non-matching plates, and an overcooked turkey, while struggling for room at the table? Different sized glasses, with cheap wine and Dad already looking forward to sleep after the meal?

This is reality versus fantasy, and you should become aware of this. Comparing yourself to others is dangerous, especially when their *perceived* reality may not be their *actual* reality, just what they have created on social media. A lot of arguments are reported to occur at Christmas, perhaps this is the reason.

Those who seek validation via social media may find it more difficult to find happiness in the moment. The desire for "Likes" on Facebook for example. Perhaps try this; do not check how many you receive. The problem with this is that your validation and acceptance by others is in a future time – the time you reach a certain number of likes, not the present moment.

The issue with this is, again, it is a never-ending search. Do you ask these questions?
- Why did this post get fewer likes than the other?
- Why did person X not like it? Have I offended them?
- I must ask them, but no, if they are offended then that's their problem.
- Why has NO-ONE liked it?

Can you see how these questions are all framed around negatives and there is never a happy outcome to be achieved.

Now consider for a moment the following, and the same can be applied if someone has ignored your call, text, or email:
- What is that person currently going through?
- Have they just had some bad news?
- Are they just busy?

Ultimately, it is rarely personal against you. Ask yourself the question, have I done anything to upset that person?

If you have had to ask yourself that question the answer is almost certainly NO. How many times has this happened to you? What has been the outcome? Most likely a message saying:
- Sorry, I saw this and forgot to reply.
- Things have been busy.
- I never saw this.

Did you feel ok afterwards? Relieved? Or did you just carry on as if nothing had happened? Try to project yourself forward to this point, thinking, it will be ok in the end; adopt the future you mindset.

It is important that you are happy with what you have, for if you are not happy with what you have, you will also not be happy with what you achieve in the future. Be honest with yourself and be genuine and authentic in what you project on social media and just take everything you see from others with a pinch of salt.

The dream life is not necessarily about material objects such as fancy cars, huge mansions, and yachts (incidentally, there is a famous quote concerning yachts):

"The 2 happiest days of a boat owners' life is the day they buy it and the day they sell it."

The dream life is primarily about being happy and grateful for what you have, right now.

"If you would not swap your family, friends, children, pet, home, etc for "all the money in the world" then you are already rich. Do not lose them in pursuit of your goals."

Your goals and being aware of what you already have.
Let us finish this chapter with a short story from Courtney Carver, www.bemorewithless.com
"An American investment banker was at the pier of a small coastal Mexican village when a small boat with just one fisherman docked. Inside the small boat were several large yellowfin tuna.

The American complimented the Mexican on the quality of his fish and asked how long it took to catch them.

The Mexican replied, "only a little while.

The American then asked, "why didn't he stay out longer and catch more fish?"

The Mexican said he had enough to support his family's immediate needs. The American then asked, "but what do you do with the rest of your time?"

The Mexican fisherman said, "I sleep late, fish a little, play with my children, take siestas with my wife, Maria, stroll into the village each evening where I sip wine, and play the guitar with my amigos. I have a full and busy life."

The American scoffed, "I am a Harvard MBA and could help you. You should spend more time fishing and with the proceeds, buy a bigger boat. With the proceeds from the bigger boat, you could buy several boats, eventually, you would have a fleet of fishing boats. Instead of selling your catch to a middleman, you would sell directly to the processor, eventually opening your own cannery.

You would control the product, processing, and distribution. You would need to leave this small coastal fishing village and move to Mexico City, then LA and eventually New York City, where you will run your expanding enterprise."

The Mexican fisherman asked, "But, how long will this all take?"

To which the American replied, "15 – 20 years."

"But what then?" Asked the Mexican.
The American laughed and said, "That's the best part. When the time is right you would announce an IPO and sell your company stock to the public and become very rich, you would make millions!"

"Millions – then what?"

The American said, "Then you would retire. Move to a small coastal fishing village where you would sleep late, fish a little, play with your kids, take siestas with your wife, stroll to the village in the evenings where you could sip wine and play your guitar with your amigos."

Be careful what you wish for and what your goals are – the journey, again, is the most important part.

Procrastination

"It doesn't matter how slowly you go as long as you do not stop"
Confucius

Now, don't be tempted to read this chapter later :-)

Just think for a moment that you are the future version of yourself and it's 5 years from now. How are you going to feel if you have followed your advice? How will you feel if you have not? What would that future you say to you right now – go ahead and visualise this for a second.

Procrastination can be a real blocker to you following this plan and making your life what you want it to be. Taking just one example, in your working life – consider the following:

It is Thursday, you have done a full day's work and you have just received notice that you need to produce a report which must be completed by 5 o'clock tomorrow. It is going to take you about 3 to 4 hours.

Option 1
- You stop working now, watch some TV and relax because after all, your working day is done.
- Tomorrow you sit down to start it and a few things come up which you were not expecting which results in you finalising the report at 1655 on a Friday evening.
- The result has been a stressful day and you do not feel like you have checked the report thoroughly.
- The other tasks that came in during the day you completed but were average at best as they did not have your full attention.
- You worry about your boss's reaction all weekend.

Option 2 – You ask Frankie – what would the "Tomorrow You" want you to do right now?
- You decide to work that little bit extra tonight up until maybe 7 o'clock or 8 o'clock.
- You complete it to 90% of your usual standard.

- You do not have to wake too early the next day and spend 30 minutes at your leisure to review and make the relevant tweaks to get it to your standard.
- Have a more relaxing day, dealing with day-to-day issues that arise.
- You get the report to your boss early afternoon, they have a chance to review and praise you to say that is exactly what they need.
- You enjoy a relaxing weekend.

The question to be asked ahead of this decision is "What would Frankie want/say?" Would Frankie (you), be happier tomorrow if you acted or did not? The above example is clear and getting into that mentality can help you to be more productive, giving you the chance of some downtime or a reward later.

This applies to non-work also:
- Tidying the house.
- Cutting the grass.
- Finishing the website you are building.
- Backing up billions of photos from old laptops (a furlough task of mine).

"Tomorrow, will you (Frankie) be happier or less happy if you do this now?"

Focus on the outcome, not the doing.
The importance is not to focus on the "doing part" but instead on the outcome. In our example above, do not think that it's 3 or 4 hours of hard work ahead, but instead on the feeling of accomplishment, the resulting payment you will receive, praise, or whatever the end outcome is.

If there is no good outcome, it begs the question of if it is worth doing. If it is work-related and something you *must* do, you need to change your outlook to being something you *want* to do, rather than you *have* to do. This is all about re-framing the situation.

As a species, we hate being told what to do and this probably stems from childhood or being governed by what we can do and when; now we have independence, we do not like to be told. If you have kids think about that; you are going to the park with them, but they don't want to walk, telling them they have to will probably result in conflict, whereas convincing them of the fun they are going to have when they get there will get a more favourable result.

I believe it is important that management styles adhere to this way of thinking; bringing employees into the decision-making process rather than autocratically making them do things results in a far more collaborative approach, with shared accountability, investment in the outcome, and more enthusiasm in the journey. Not to mention the fact that they are far more likely to have valuable input which will improve the outcome.

"Leaders who don't listen will eventually be surrounded by people who have nothing to say", *Andy Stanley*

Continuing with our example above, there are 2 ways to look at it.
View 1
- My boss needs this report. I think it is pointless and I do not want to do it.
- There are so many other things I could be doing.
- Why can't they just do it themselves?
- I have never done this before so how can I be expected to do it correctly?
- They can have it at 1655 tomorrow afternoon – last minute…I am not impressed.

View 2

- There must be importance around this.
- I want to get this done because the message I can create through it is an important one.
- My boss is already happy with me, let's push that higher.
- This is the first report of this nature that I have done, I should attempt to create it as a template whilst doing this so that it can speed up the process the next time.
- If I get this done ahead of time, especially given the short notice, my boss will be happy.

I think it is quite clear which is the most positive and most likely to result in a happier (and more successful) you. Also, which report is going to be the best? And which version of Frankie will be the boss of the future and which will be almost identical in the future as they are now? (assuming they have managed to keep their job).

"It is important to view it as 'I want to' rather than 'I have to'. This slight change in thinking is incredibly powerful."

I travel a lot for my job and I also have a lot of work to do outside of travelling or meetings. If I have work to do for the next day, or even later that week, I will get to the hotel and either complete the work or at least "break the back of it". It gives a great sense of achievement and makes my life easier in the coming days – it is then time to relax and switch off, which is also made easier once complete. **Make the task the *outcome* rather than the *work*, focus on that outcome but first decide if that is an outcome that you want.**

If you have a very lengthy document, report, presentation, business plan etc to create, there are 2 ways to approach this.

Option 1

Spend hours thinking about it, planning, outlining the approach and the resources. Put a completion plan together and focus on how you can do it.

Option 2

Start! Do the minimum – but do it now.

Now, this may sound like option 2 is the easiest but it will produce the worst result. Not so, because I am not quite finished. For this, I wish to discuss perfection.

Progress, not Perfection

"Practice Makes Progress", My Kids

Perfection does not exist; you will never get 100% perfection in what you do because there is always room for improvement. What if the following is true?

- 99% perfection or at least striving to get there is going to take you 8 hours.
- But getting to say 80% perfection is going to take you 2 hours, do that and get it to 80%

You will get a sense of achievement and a particularly good sense of well-being. Then have a break from it, go away, go for a walk or just relax. After a short while, go back and make those tweaks to bring that to fruition to get closer to that 100%. This approach gets you to the same result but for a significantly less amount of time invested and a lot less stress. This arguably gives better results because the time you save can be used to review and add additional content you may not have thought about in the frantic alternative.

"Striving for something that cannot be achieved is the fast track to unhappiness".

Framing

What is this? A good example of this is the "Holiday Blues". If you are returning from holiday, you anticipate this which means you may start thinking and worrying about this towards the end of the holiday, spoiling the last few days. In the past I have been working in a stressful environment which I have not enjoyed and caused me a great deal of anxiety; on one holiday, the anxiety started a whole 7 days before returning. I had thoughts like "this time next week I will be at work."

Now, this was indicative of a bad mindset and yes, granted, a bad work environment that had to be changed, but the point is it was made worse by continually thinking those thoughts.

"Never regret your decisions; if you are not happy, change the situation but do not live with regret."

You need to make returning from holiday more attractive than staying. For example, instead of thinking:

"I am going to miss the hotel and not having to work. Instead, I am going to have to get up in the cold weather at 7 am on Monday and go to work."

Reframe this to:

"This has been a great break with the family and the weather has been great – I am really lucky. I cannot wait to get back to see other family members, we are going to go for a long walk in the country the weekend after we get back.
I am going to suggest the ideas for change at work that I have been thinking about by the pool, which could result in a pay rise and greater job satisfaction. Either way, I want to get back to progress my career and this holiday will be repeated next year as a reward for all of my hard work."

Self Improvement.

What do you want to do in life? Do you want to be a master chess player, a master violinist or is it something related to your job?

Whatever it is you can achieve it if you set your mind to it and take that all-important first step.

In a work environment, perhaps you wish to become the leader of the company or department so how do you do it? You plan.

Look at the person who does this best:
- How do they act?
- How do they dress?
- What do they do differently to others?
- How do they treat others?

You can learn from them from afar and you may also be surprised to hear that they will most likely also help you directly. Most people are happy to help, so approaching that person and asking for guidance is more likely to be met with a positive outcome (especially if you follow the guidance in the story about the farmer in the chapter "Positive Thinking").

Try this. For the person who does the role that you want, or the person who is at the top of their chosen discipline, whose footsteps you would like to follow, spend some time and analyse their career path.

For business or career, LinkedIn may be a good place to start or the internet if they are famous, and document how they got to where they are. What jobs or training did they do, year by year, to get where they are?

Now put this plan down into what you are going to do. What roles will take you to the dream role? What training do you need and what experience?

You will now have a plan over a duration of time which may be 20 years, 10 years, 1 year or less, depending on the goal. Make it achievable and realistic but big enough that it excites you.

The First Step
Once you have a plan, which may cover the next 5 years, the most important is the first step – what can you do today that can point you in that right direction?

"The worst thing you can do is to dream about that but do nothing about it – because in 5 years you will be in the same position – decide consciously to invest your time now."

Is there any online training you can register for? Is there a mentor that you can speak to for guidance?

If it is work-related, have you had ideas as to how the company could work better and if so, have you communicated these? If not, start here and work on a plan, this will get you noticed as well as being a great value add to the company that you work for.

Do more than you are paid to do.
I have always applied this throughout my career. Try to never get tied up in "this is my job and that's not my job so, therefore, I'm not going to do it". Be a team player and look out for the wellbeing of your colleagues – but do this from the heart and not because you feel that you must; be genuine.

During recent years I have become a "mental health buddy" at work, supporting colleagues who may need help – this is a real eye-opening experience and it is so important these days to keep checking in with people, to make sure that they are ok. After all, "It's ok, not to be ok".

I have also recently completed a short "Suicide Prevention" – this is free to do and I encourage everyone to do it. It takes only 20 minutes and could very well save someone's life. Details can be found in the resources section.

Ultimately, in work or anywhere:

"BE KIND AND AWARE OF OTHERS"

More and more the measure of a person is becoming far less about achievement and more about how nice/kind they are. We have seen a massive switch in the world recently and thankfully mental health is being brought to the forefront.

It is no longer the taboo subject that it once was; help and support is more readily available which is excellent.

Always try to be aware of what impact your actions have on others, you will find that kindness projected outwards tends to come back to you.

What do you want to learn and understand? You really can pick anything you like – resources are out there.

It is said that with learning, you never go back:

"A mind that is stretched by a new experience can never go back to its old dimensions.", *Oliver Wendell Holmes*

Refer back to your obituary and understand what it is that you would like your message to be and therefore which area of education would benefit you?

"The starting point and the destination are vital, but so too are regular reviews."

The whole point of the reviews detailed in part One is to make sure that you stay on track.

What happens on a flight from an airliner? The Captain knows where the starting point is and where the destination is with a flight path showing the route.

We have previously mentioned this quote, but it is very relevant here:

"All airplanes are off course 99% of the time. The purpose and role of the pilot and the avionics is to continually bring the plane back on course so that it arrives on schedule at its destination"
Brian Tracey

Applying this analogy to your goals, you need regular checkpoints throughout your journey to ensure that you are moving in the right direction hence the importance of the review sheets. (It also means you can enjoy the journey due to being aware you have a framework surrounding your plans.) It also means that you can, intentionally or otherwise, deviate but still enjoy the journey and ultimately get to the same place.

Take a basic example of running the London Marathon next year. You decide that you need to run 4 times per week, for an increased duration on each occasion.

You could miss one week with the promise to get back on track, but before you consciously know it, it has been 2 months and you did not realise consciously how many sessions you have missed.

Doing the weekly and monthly reviews gives you accountability and therefore increases your chance of sticking to the plan.
For the right reasons and in the right way.
Whatever you do to progress, if you are doing it for the right reasons and not to the detriment of others, then you will be able to lead a successful and fulfilling life. This means living true to your values and your obituary should be consistent with this.

In business there is a saying that working your way up the ladder with care and respect for everybody else, (you will also find that many will reciprocate and you help each other) it will mean there will be a lot of people to catch you should you fall. However, the converse is also true, if you get up that ladder by treating people badly with no respect and doing things at the detriment to their progression, there will be very few people there to catch you. Which position would you prefer to be in?

Be Kind
I think the most important thing in life is to help others and to be kind. You can tell a lot about a person by observing them and what they do. If 100 people meet you, there are 100 versions of you existing in the world, make sure that this is always positive.

One of my Dad's sayings is:
"If you have to tell people how important you are, you are not as important as you think you are."

I think this is so true – you are no more important than anyone else, but also, nor are they.

For Christmas, a couple of years back, my mum had written a series of quotes in a notebook for me. It was an incredible gift and I keep it with me to this day. One of the quotes was:

"You can get what you want/need, by helping as many other people as possible to get what they want/need." Zig Ziglar (...and my Mum)
Observing people gives you a good indication of their character. Especially when you observe **how they treat people when they do not need to be nice to them.**

This is an especially important point – one of the worst examples of this is in a restaurant. Have you noticed some people allow the kind person serving them, to put the food or drink down and do not so much as acknowledge this? It's almost as if they view themselves as superior. But you know what, that person is doing a job to earn money, just the same as the diner most likely has to. On the other hand, observe the people who make a point of thanking them, they acknowledge that they are no better or worse, no more or less important, and no more or less worthy, because, simply, they aren't.

I believe that we are all connected and therefore harming anyone is ultimately harming the collective and therefore yourself.

If you truly believe the above then it does highlight the ridiculousness of prejudice such as racism; the world would be a far better place if we could accept this and live together in peace.

Mindfulness

**"I have so much to accomplish today that I must meditate for
two hours instead of one"**
Mahatma Gandhi

This chapter is around the mindfulness that we have touched on briefly, one thing that we try and get across in this book is the fact that you should make decisions consciously, don't just do what your subconscious tells you but think about what you are doing.

One of the problems we get into these days is doing things that potentially we will regret when we look back on them. When we do look back on our life as per the previous chapters around the past 5 years there are a lot of things that we would have done differently now.

We need to break that subconscious cycle and one way we can do that is with meditation.

"Frankie is this future person, who will be wishing you had done things differently (exactly as you are now) but with the benefit of hindsight."

A lot of people do not meditate and what puts them off is they say they don't have time. One thing you can try is to incorporate it into your daily life; something that hopefully most of us do every day is to have a shower, so meditate in the shower.

Shower Meditation
Shower in the normal way but at the end when you just do not want to get out of the nice warm water, envisage yourself as a glass vase shape of yourself which is full of water that has all of the remnants of broken night's sleep and worries and general junk. Imagine standing under a wonderful waterfall, with the crystal-clear water falling on top of you.

Allow that to come down and allow the vision of the "less than pure water" to flow out of your body, washed out by the clean water. Once empty allow the water to fall through the opening in your head, filling you up.

Be aware of the feeling as it works up your ankles, calves and thighs - all the way through your body until you feel that it is overflowing at the top, have that image of that crystal clear water you find at the waterfall at the bottom of the mountain - it's crystal clear and almost forms a bright light surrounding and protecting you as it overflows.

This is a completely different self-image of you from a few minutes earlier. You are now this radiant crystal-clear vessel, filled and ready for the day ahead. It gives you a good feeling to go out into the day with but also enables you to stop thinking albeit for a very short period, so it gives your mind a rest which is a very important thing.

Meditation is something that you should try to bring into your life as much as possible. The focusing of the mind on something as simple as breathing can assist you to be mindful and switch off from the overwhelming thoughts that you may have. Remember, thoughts are what give power, therefore reducing thoughts, reduces the power and thus the effect they can have on you.

Bringing your attention to your breath, even for 10 minutes, can have a profound effect. Try this:
-   Find a quiet place where you will not be disturbed.
-   Close your eyes.
-   Breathe in through your nose to the count of 5
-   Hold for 5.
-   Breath out through your mouth to the count of 5
-   Hold for 5.
-   If you find your mind wandering, this is ok, just bring it back to the breath when you realise.
-   Do this for 5 minutes to start with, then build up to as long as you are comfortable.
-   Count out loud if it helps you.

There are several meditation apps out there, such as:
- Calm.
- Headspace.

There is a quote that says:
"I have so much to accomplish today that I must meditate for two hours instead of one" - *Mahatma Gandhi*

This quote highlights the fact that if you feel you don't have time to meditate, you need it more than ever. Consider how many times in a day that you do switch off, even for 5 minutes.

"Feelings come and go like clouds in a windy sky. Conscious breathing is my anchor.", Thich Nhat Hahn

Meditation can be done in several ways and there is no right or wrong way. The key is to stop your mind from racing and give it a little quiet time.

Healthline.com shows the following benefits to meditation:
- Reduce Stress.
- Control Anxiety.
- Promotes emotional health.
- Enhances self-awareness.
- Lengthens attention span.
- May reduce age-related memory loss.
- Can generate kindness.
- May help fight addictions.
- Improves sleep.
- Helps control pain.
- Can decrease blood pressure.
- Accessible anywhere.

Tea Meditation

Another meditation you may find useful is around tea. The University of Newcastle Upon Tyne, 29 December 2020, published research around the health benefits of tea, around the attention span for elderly people. (https://bit.ly/2PcqSka)

This study revolved around brain function and attention span *"In tests, they showed better accuracy and speed of reaction which could help in daily activities such as completing a jigsaw, sewing or driving a car."*

Dr Edward Okello, Principle investigator said *"the skills we see maintained in this group of very old may not only be due to the compounds present in tea, but it may also be the rituals of making a pot of tea or sharing a chat over a cup of tea are just as important."*

I believe that this is due to the ritual more than the ingredients. Tibetan monks have this ritual and can be a good way to quieten the mind.

The meditation is amazingly simple. Make the tea in your usual way, best in a pot, but do each step consciously. Focus on each stage, do it with purpose and for the act itself. For example:
- Boil the water.
- Put a small amount of boiling water in the pot and use it to rinse, this warms the teapot.
- Put in the teabag(s).
- Put in the boiling water.
- Allow brewing for 3-4 minutes while focusing on the teapot and what is happening within.
- Add milk to the cup.
- Pour the tea, observing the way it flows, mixes and steams.
- Take some quiet time to drink, taking notice of the flavour, heat and feeling that you experience.

The whole meditation can be very beneficial, but make sure that you do it with full attention – focus 100% on this task and you quieten the mind.

NB: *This is for the benefit of Andy, a good friend of mine.* I know that the debate of whether you should make tea in a teapot or a mug as well as whether the milk goes in first is a source of massive debate across social platforms.

Allow me to give my humble opinion.
If making tea in a cup only, milk should go in last as it blocks the holes in the teabag. If it is being made the **correct** way :-), in a pot, then the milk goes into the cup first.

The reason for this is based in history. Back when teacups were fine china, the milk was put in first to make sure that the boiling water did not crack the cup.

So now you know…..

Walking Meditation
Another meditation that I carry out is in nature, walking. This can be done anywhere and at any time.

Quite simply, find the number of steps that you are comfortable with for breathing in, holding and breathing out. For example, focus on your breath and the steps:
- Breath in for 5 steps.
- Hold for 5 steps.
- Breath out of 5 steps.

For each step, be aware of the feeling and any sounds that you hear. Try to recognise as many sounds as you can, birds, animals, wind in the trees.

It doesn't matter if you lose count, start again, or overcount. The important part is that you are focussing on your breath and the steps; focusing on nature and not on stresses and worries.

This has the obvious benefit also of exercise and being in the outdoors – observe nature, hug a tree, whatever is needed and works for you.

Remember, there is no right and wrong way to meditate – all meditation is, is bringing your attention to something other than your thoughts.

After a meditation, you may feel like you have failed because you instantly go back to thinking – this is fine. The point is that for that period, your mind was getting a break. Thoughts constantly enter your mind, the key is to acknowledge them, let them go and not dwell on them.

Daily Routine

"You'll never change your life until you change something you do daily. The secret of your success is found in your daily routine"

John C. Maxwell

We have referred to the daily routine several times and this routine is quite important to break cycles and achieve the life you want. As part of our daily routine, we carry out the following tasks:

- As many times as you remember, observe your thoughts – if you are sitting in a meeting, take the time to watch yourself from a point on the opposite wall and think:
    - I am in this meeting with some especially important people.
    - I am changing the outcome of this meeting.
    - I am worried about a part of it, but it is going to be ok because I am handling it just fine.
- If you are working in the outdoors, stop to reflect on nature, the people around you, the sounds, the smells – for that short time, be aware of YOU, and where you are.
- If you feel overwhelmed, STOP. Float out of your body and watch yourself from above – watch how you are worrying/anxious etc – viewing from the 3rd person perspective is immensely powerful as we have already explained.
- Smile at at least one stranger.
    - This may seem strange, however, that smile or warmth shown to someone may make all the difference in the world to them.
- Strike up a conversation with at least one stranger.
    - As per the last point – you never know that interaction may be enough to prevent them from doing something bad that they had planned for someone, or themselves.
        - Again, this may sound farfetched, however, you never know what is going on in other people's lives.
- Always be approachable and willing to help or listen to anyone – it really can make a difference to that person.

- Write down 3 things per day that you are grateful for and ensure you keep them so that you can look back on them when you need a lift.
  - Use them in your life story, focus on them and be amazed when more positive events occur.
- Create a folder in your Email for positive things. Whenever you get praise at work or anything nice is said about you on email, save it in that folder – you will find the more you focus on this, the more positivity comes your way – it works!
- Record any lessons that you have learned that day.
- Carry out meditation in the shower, walking or drinking tea.
- Read uplifting stories, check out Ione Butlers Uplifting Stories, https://amzn.to/3wXazla
  - Read one per day.

Avoid self-promotion – in other words, if you help someone who was injured, donated to charity, or did something that sometimes others have not – do not publicise it. Do not go straight to social media and tell people what you have done – if you do, you have carried out that kind act for one reason – yourself.

This is never looked upon favourably anyway – someone who does this and then shouts about it, has done this for that exact reason. Be discreet in your assistance, give to charity privately, help someone and keep it to yourself; if not for any other reason than by saying it to others, it proves you did it just for their acceptance. The gratitude will come from the recipient, not those hearing about it.

Always try to ensure that you are doing the right thing for yourself and others. For example, if you are currently bullying or victimising someone at work or otherwise, just know this; you cannot do a bad thing to another without it negatively impacting yourself. Not to mention the fact that, from a selfish perspective, what if:

- That person harms themselves or takes their own life, how would you feel then?
- That person becomes your boss.

There is ALWAYS a right way and a wrong way. If you are not sure which is the right way, Ask Frankie – the advisors should keep you right.

The basis of this book is to get you to start thinking about every decision you make. We have been doing this for several years now and it becomes second nature – but in the early stages think - "what would the future you (Frankie) think?"

Consciously making every decision can change your life for the better, you become your boss and take total responsibility for your life.

Summary and Next steps

"You can only control *your* thoughts and *your* actions, so please, control wisely"
Gareth Lewis and Steven Eddy (That's us by the way)

Is the life you have painted in this book one that you would like?

Do the sacrifices you have to make seem easily achieved and possible?

If the answer to both questions is yes, then congratulations you have the vision and incentive to make it happen.

You need to work on that outcome being bigger and better, and not focus on the detail of the steps you need to take between here and there. Little steps will get you to where you want to be you just have to constantly think about what that is.

The wonderful thing is that if you reverse those bad decisions from day one, it allows you, in five years, to completely transform your life as well as your outlook on life. What have you got to lose?

Reading this book does not take a long time. This is deliberate because we prefer that it is read in one sitting and therefore becomes that bit more achievable.

The hard work for you is only to decide what you want to do, write it down and then check in with yourself and your team daily, weekly and monthly as per section 1.

Now, please ask yourself these 2 questions:
If you had done this 5 years ago, what would life be like now?

If you do what you have noted down here, in five years is that something you want?

Or do you want to find this book in 5 years and think – "Damn, I wish I had done this". 5 years is not a long time to realise the life of your dreams. Start now – plan now and start recording your progress. You will begin to see real positive changes much sooner.

So, take that first step to complete the documents, put the information into the spreadsheet if you have not already done so and see what that "Future You" looks like. Constantly check in with yourself and ask if the future you (Frankie) would be happier or less happy if you took this action.

I said previously that the 'Future You' is a minute, a day, a week, a month, a year, a decade in the future. "I'll be happy if I get that done now", "will you be happier if you painted that room tonight rather than leave it for tomorrow".

Lastly, do not forget that happiness is not a destination but the journey to that destination, set the goals that excite you but also will have a pleasurable journey, review regularly, and above all enjoy that journey.

We wish you all the luck in the world.

The community (a private Facebook group) is an interactive group where members can help each other with topics relating to the book or any other thoughts, you can find this group on our facebook page.

Let's work together to make our worlds a better place for each other.

Peace and Love.

Frankie x

Additional Info and Resources

> "Live as if you were to die tomorrow. Learn as if you were to live forever"
> Mahatma Gandhi

We love to receive feedback and so please see our contact details below on email and social media.

Gareth Lewis
LinkedIn - https://www.linkedin.com/in/garethlewissap
Clubhouse - @garethlewis-sap

Both Authors
Email - info@ask-frankie.com
Facebook - fb.me/thefutureyou1

Recommended Reading

We have mentioned several different resources throughout this book, and we would like to bring all of this together.

Ione Butler, Uplifting Stories, https://amzn.to/34ngdqJ
- Amazing stories to lift you. Compiled by the founder of www.upliftingcontent.com
- m.facebook.com/upliftingcontent
- www.ionebutler.com
- Youtube.com/ionebutler
- Youtube.com/upliftingcontent
- Instagram.com/upliftingcontent
- Instagram.com/ionebutler
- Twitter.com/upliftingcont
- Twittercom/ionebutler

Matthew Pollard, The Introverts Edge, https://amzn.to/3wBx5WQ
- Perfect for anyone who is, or wished to be in sales but struggles with confidence.
- Instagram
- Twitter
- Facebook

Cian Mcloughlin, Rebirth of a Salesman, https://amzn.to/3vj7t0B
- For anyone in business and wanting to be, this is a seriously important read – depicts the move to a more authentic approach to sales and therefore more genuine.

Raphael Rowe, Notorious, https://amzn.to/3fN5QBN
- Feel like the odds are stacked against you?
- Does your situation seem desperate?
- Read this and be truly inspired by Raphael Rowe.
- I loved this book and proves that with the right mindset you can overcome any issue or injustice.

Ashley Kesner, Free Your Ghost. www.freeyourghost.com
- Ashley is an inspirational connection of mine
- She specialises in addiction, specifically around alcohol.
- Ashley has created a wonderful community.
- Her message resonates with the basis of this book, she refers to thinking of the last drink, not the first one. In other words, how do you feel at that future point?

Ania Halama, Rebels Guide to Spirituality, https://amzn.to/2SpFs94
- A very honest and open account of her life.
- Packed with tips around healing and improving yourself through various practices.

Paul Mort, Paul Mort Will Save Your Life, https://amzn.to/3zFra5j
- Fantastic listen – from the heart and no holds barred.
- Local to us, North East.
- Just listen to it – highly recommended

Richard Wiseman, The Luck Factor, https://amzn.to/2RQQowm
- A fascinating account of whether there is such a thing as lucky and unlucky people.

Rob Moore, Money, https://amzn.to/3yC69bc
- Understand the mechanics behind money
- "Money is a game you can win. First, understand the rules with this extraordinary bestseller."

Jim Kwik, Limitless, https://amzn.to/3fnL4d6
- Simply life-changing. Improve your memory or increase your reading speed.

- I have raised my reading speed from 200 words per minute to 480 and I am still practising
- I comprehend the information a lot more and get an overall greater enjoyment out of reading.

Matthew Michalewicz- Life in Half a Second, ttps://amzn.to/3fPZD7Y
- Amazing and fascinating content that puts a lot of issues into perspective.

Napoleon Hill, Think and Grow Rich https://amzn.to/3fQtJZh
- An all-time classic that has stood the test of time.

Useful Links
Suicide Prevention Training
- https://www.ohana.ie/
- 20 Minute, free course, to assist you in how to handle the situation

NHS – Mental Health Resources
- https://www.nhs.uk/conditions/stress-anxiety-depression/mental-health-helplines/

Mind – Mental Health Resource
- https://www.mind.org.uk/

Printed in Great Britain
by Amazon